Acclaim for Gary Moore

Gary Moore is a believer who takes the idea of stewardship to unexpected lengths.

Money Magazine
November 1998

You, Gary, make convincing economic and moral arguments, which, as you know, are sometimes treated mistakenly as mutually contradictory.

William J. Bennett
former Secretary of Education
and author of *The Book of Virtues*

My friend Gary Moore knows the truth that high ethical and spiritual principles and generosity lead to prosperity.

Sir John M. Templeton
Founder, the Templeton Mutual Funds

Since I came to know him in 1992, Gary has advocated some rather contrarian views on the economy, which have proven to be excellent counsel. He continues to provide a wise, Judeo-Christian based perspective, which I value.

Dick Towner
Director of Financial Ministries
the sixteen-thousand-attendee Willow Creek Community Church

D1590044

Epigraph

A Gold Mine Concerning Money, Life, and a Time When We Will No Longer Value Either

Again, [the kingdom of heaven] will be like a man going on a journey, who called his servants and entrusted his property to them. To one he gave five talents of money, to another two talents, and to another one talent, each according to his ability. Then he went on his journey. The man who had received the five talents went at once and put his money to work and gained five more. So also, the one with the two talents gained two more. But the man who had received the one talent went off, dug a hole in the ground and hid his master's money.

After a long time the master of those servants returned and settled accounts with them. The man who had received the five talents brought the other five. "Master," he said, "you entrusted me with five talents. See, I have gained five more."

His master replied, "Well done, good and faithful servant! You have been faithful with a few things; I will put you in charge of many things. Come and share your master's happiness!"

The man with the two talents also came. "Master," he said, "you entrusted me with two talents; see, I have gained two more."

His master replied, "Well done, good and faithful servant! You have been faithful with a few things; I will put you in charge of many things. Come and share your master's happiness!"

Then the man who had received the one talent came. "Master," he said, "I knew that you are a hard man, harvesting where you have not sown and gathering where you have not scattered seed. So I was afraid and went out and hid your talent in the ground. See, here is what belongs to you."

His master replied, "You wicked, lazy servant! So you knew that I harvest where I have not sown and gather where I have not scattered seed? Well then, you should have put my money on deposit with the bankers, so that when I returned I would have received it back with interest.

"Take the talent from him and give it to the one who has the ten talents. For everyone who has will be given more, and he will have an abundance. Whoever does not have, even what he has will be taken from him. And throw that worthless servant outside, into the darkness, where there will be weeping and gnashing of teeth."

JESUS OF NAZARETH
MATTHEW 25:14–30

END-TIMES MONEY MANAGEMENT

PROTECTING YOUR RESOURCES WITHOUT LOSING YOUR SOUL

GARY MOORE

ZondervanPublishingHouse
Grand Rapids, Michigan

A Division of HarperCollins*Publishers*

Note:

As he wrote this book, Gary Moore was guided by the spirit of this passage from Paul Johnson, a theologian whose work often appears in the *Wall Street Journal:*

There are those writers who have not sought to tell the world what to do, to create Utopias out of their own unaided intellects and incited people into trying to bring them about, but instead have simply set themselves to portray God's universe and his people in loving words. *They will have a smooth passage through the storms of that tremendous judgment day.* These are writers who, by their modest genius have sought chiefly to enable their readers to see God's creation with fresh eyes—have taught us to look, again and again, at the world around us and the way humans behave. Such writers are dear to God.[1]

But mark this: There will be terrible times in the last days. People will be lovers of themselves, lovers of money ... having a form of godliness but denying its power.

SAINT PAUL
2 TIMOTHY 3:1–2, 5

End-Times Money Management
Copyright © 1999 by Gary D. Moore

Requests for information should be addressed to:

ZondervanPublishingHouse
Grand Rapids, Michigan 49530

Library of Congress Cataloging-in-Publication Data

Moore, Gary D.
    End-times money management : protecting your resources without losing your soul / Gary Moore.
      p.   cm.
      ISBN 0-310-22360-1 (softcover)
    1. Finance, Personal—Religious aspects—Christianity. 2. Investments—Religious aspects—
Christianity I. Title.
HG179.M613 1998
332.024—dc21   98-46641
                                                                                CIP

Interior design by Sherri L. Hoffman
Printed in the United States of America

99 00 01 02 03 04 05 /❖ DC/ 10 9 8 7 6 5 4 3 2 1

Dedication

To Skip, my old friend and constant reminder that the poor are often the richest in dreams, especially for their children and grandchildren. You told me once that when we were young, I used to go to church to learn about God but you were already relying on God just to get through each day. As I grow older, I am beginning to understand your perspective. God now seems so very real, not because the church taught me as much but because life has taught me as much.

Contents

Introduction

The Greatest Risk-Reward Calculation
of All Time

*In an age in which investing seems to have transubstantiated
into pop religion, high-profile Wall Street soothsayers serve as
our spiritual guides. Each day, they tell Main Street why the
market soared or swooned, as well as what might happen
tomorrow and beyond. And Main Street listens.*

U.S. NEWS & WORLD REPORT

I grew up on a remote farm in central Kentucky. We were
poor. We rarely took a vacation or even a day just to enjoy
life. My father was loving but I hardly knew him. He was a stoic
type who always seemed to have two or three things going in order
to help us achieve that Great American Dream. That meant I got to
live a monastic existence from Monday to Saturday as I cared for
the family farm. But we always assumed that one day we would
"make it" and begin to live. As I was used to being alone, I didn't
really feel the enormous irony when Dad died of cancer just a few
months before he was to retire.

Sundays always revolved around church. My parents once took me
to services for six years without missing a Sunday. But my life quickly
began to reflect that old saying that if you think going to church makes
you a Christian, sit in a garage and see if you become a car.

In 1968 I left the farm and entered the University of Kentucky
to study political science. I had an uncle who was a high-ranking
official in Washington, and after spending a little time there I had

been tempted to save the world through politics. For years I had slept beneath a poster of the Capitol dome. There was a quote on the poster that simply said, "Here, sir, the people govern."

You may remember that 1968 was the year of the Tet Offensive in Vietnam, the riots surrounding the Democratic convention in Chicago, and the assassinations of Martin Luther King and Bobby Kennedy. This idealistic farm boy hardly knew what hit him. I remember watching as they carried candles in the darkness in front of my dormitory. I appeared on front pages around the country when a photographer captured me looking at the torched remains of my ROTC building. And like most of my fellow baby boomers, I grew rather skeptical of that institution we call government.

As a conservative, I had always known that Karl Marx had established a secular religion called communism. That is, he worshiped the community at the expense of the individual citizen. But as I took a few political science courses, I was introduced to a philosopher named Ayn Rand. She had created a secular religion called objectivism. That is, she worshiped the "objective" reasoning of the individual rather than the dictates of government officials. So while Karl Marx and communists put their faith in government, Ayn Rand condemned it, a belief of many Americans we call libertarians.

Yet like Marx, Rand also hated Christianity and its Bible. After all, if Christians place less than faith in government, Saint Paul still tells us in the book of Romans to respect government and to pay our taxes, as we have nothing to fear from authority—assuming we behave ourselves. And if our own thinking is sufficient, as Rand believed, why do we need the revelations of the Bible?

When the *Economist* magazine recently listed the most influential thinkers in our world, Rand was the only woman it mentioned. Alan Greenspan, the head of the Federal Reserve Board, literally sat at her feet as a disciple during the sixties. When junk-bond king Michael Milken went to prison, he spent his time rereading the gospel of Ayn Rand. Arnold Schwartzeneggar routinely testifies that her thinking changed his life. Her thinking has influenced millions who do not even know that her first name is spelled *A-y-n* rather than *A-n-n*. I believe this includes some ministry leaders that I have debated on Christian radio during recent years.

Yet Ayn Rand wrote her own scriptures. It is a book entitled *Atlas Shrugged*. In it she created her own secular savior, whose name was John Galt. In the last sentence of *Atlas Shrugged*, John Galt casts a new sign over the world. It is a symbol that Rand hoped would replace both the hammer and sickle and the cross. It was the sign of the dollar.

In short, Ayn Rand did not believe that the love of money is the root of all evil. In fact, she believed that the love of money—rather than the love of God and neighbor as self—is the great commandment for organizing life. One of her other books, entitled *The Virtue of Selfishness,* was a commentary on why *Atlas Shrugged* contains no story about a Good Samaritan. I noticed that when our nation recently celebrated the president's volunteerism conference in Philadelphia, Rand's disciples protested the event by carrying signs suggesting we read *Atlas Shrugged.*

Ayn Rand spoke of being buried beneath a six-foot dollar sign, just as Christians are often buried beneath the cross. And she wrote to friends that she hoped to create a new faith for people who no longer truly believed the Old One of Moses and Jesus.

As this young farm boy had grown disillusioned with government, Rand's distaste for it seemed rather logical while Vietnam, Watergate, and other events unfolded. And if I couldn't save the world through politics, why not make a few dollars for myself? So after a period as an artillery officer, I entered the world of Wall Street.

During the eighties I lived where I could make the most money. I worked for firms that would pay the most money. I invested where I could make the most money. I joined clubs where I could rub elbows with big money. And though I avoided this one temptation, I even had friends who joined churches and served ministries for the sole purpose of meeting people with a lot of money. I even remember one young broker asking our manager if he should join the Baptist church or the Episcopal church, the two richest churches in town, as if it were simply another marketing decision. They eventually decided he should split his time between the two.

In coming years I grew to know some people in *Forbes* magazine's list of the four hundred richest people in America. Bill Gates wasn't one of them, but I still grew as preoccupied with his wealth as most Americans seem today. As an aside, I might tell you that I had the privilege of speaking at a gathering of one thousand Christian stewardship leaders not long ago. The topic of the day seemed to be Mr. Gates becoming the richest man in the world. But when I asked, I discovered that very few of the stewardship leaders knew that there are eight nations on earth where over half the people live on one dollar per day or less.

It's an illusion that the superrich are as important as we imagine. Let me give you some facts. The average net worth of the four hundred members last year was $1.6 billion. That means all four hundred were worth about $640 billion. That's a lot of money. But public and private economists routinely estimate America's wealth at over $55 *trillion*. That means the people in the *Forbes* list may control a little over one percent of our nation's wealth, and probably less than one-quarter of one percent of the world's wealth. Perhaps that is why Jesus spent more time thinking about the typical steward and the "least of these," those one billion people on this planet who live on a dollar a day or less.

If you make minimum wage in the United States, you make about twenty times what those one billion people do. If you make our average wage, you make about fifty times what they do, and your wages are probably among the top one percent in human history.

I've found there's a spiritual dimension in being conscious of those numbers and facts. My clients who obsess over Mr. Gates usually feel very poor indeed. But those who keep the "least of these" in mind usually feel very blessed, or deeply contented and happy.

But to return to my journey and the late eighties: After a decade of learning with other people's money, I was a senior vice president of a major investment firm, with some money of my own. I had the corner office on the thirty-eighth floor. I looked down on the town and bay each day. I had two luxury cars. I had a thirty-foot fishing boat. I traveled the world. I thought I had gained it. But though I was the lay leader of my local church at the time, I awoke in my own bedroom one morning sobbing into my hands and asking the ancient question of Solomon: "Is this all there is?"

There's an old saying that a man leaves the home of his youth in search of God and returns home to find him. I found myself back on the farm reading the Bible of my youth. I was startled as obscure passages that I barely remembered seemed to make incredible sense. For example, I read that the fields in ancient Israel were square but the Israelites would round the corners at harvesttime. This left grain in the corners that the poor could harvest. At first that seemed illogical to a farm boy turned political analyst turned investment strategist. We moderns worship economic "efficiency." Marx seemed to whisper, "Harvest it all, pay taxes, and allow the government to send welfare checks to the poor." But Moses seemed to respond, "Won't they eventually forget how to harvest for themselves?" Rand seemed to whisper, "Harvest it all, make all you can, and let your neighbor do the same for himself." But Moses seemed to respond, "What about the neighbors who do not own land?" And Jesus seemed to sigh, "How many barns of grain will finally make you happy?"

It won't sound logical to many of us, but when the Israelites sacrificed a little, they assured a more materially abundant life for all. And that surely made everyone a little happier, or spiritually richer. That's why even George Bernard Shaw once called Jesus "a first-rate political economist." That's a rather secular appreciation of Jesus. But it and the first-rate spiritual advice I had found in Jesus' words from the mount were enough to tempt me to escape Wall Street for seminary.

As I underwent the normal psychological testing required for all seminary aspirants, I discovered I can barely see male images in inkblots. Without knowing anything of my youth, the psychologist told me about the absence of my workaholic father. He explained that since it was a loving absence, I did not harbor the anger that inner-city gang members do. Instead I was experiencing a loneliness that often drove me to seek too much approval from my peers. So I too had become a workaholic—just like my father. And I have spent many hours since wondering what Dad and I were doing that was so terribly important. I can't tell you how many of my friends relate to that. Perhaps you can as well.

By the grace of God, my church encouraged me to deal with my world rather than escape it by going to seminary. I had already started writing a pamphlet about money, which my church was going to publish. Although I had intended to give a little back to God by taking a couple of months to write it, I was drawn into two years of wrestling with God and the secular religions of politics and economics. Most of my associates and clients surely thought I had lost my mind. I found it ironic that when I had been losing my mind, they thought I was perfectly sane, but when I began to reclaim my sanity, they thought I had begun to lose my mind. I grew to appreciate that Bible verse in which God says to humanity, "My thoughts are not your thoughts."

I'm sure I nearly drove my wife crazy. Like most baby boomers, we had the majority of our savings in a retirement plan. In the two years of writing what had evolved from a pamphlet into a book, we ran through everything that was liquid, or readily convertible into cash outside of my IRA. At four o'clock one afternoon I was staring at a request form for taking money out of my plan so I could keep working on the book. I turned from my desk, looked down on the city, and began wrestling with God again. I explained that it surely wasn't good stewardship to further invade my principal. And it couldn't be the wisdom of Solomon to incur a ten percent penalty to the government for early withdrawal.

But as the tears began to flow, I heard myself saying to God, "I've found something more valuable than my retirement fund. If it takes every penny to share with others what I've learned, it all belongs to you anyway." As I turned back around, I realized it had taken me an hour to finally surrender to the God of Judeo-Christianity. I can't adequately explain with words the joy experienced when a person who has been pulled apart from three different directions finally discovers peace by committing to one.

Though it's rarely quoted by Christian financial authors and speakers, there *is* a biblical story about Job that assures God may test us with the loss of material wealth. I had started to understand that story very well. Fortunately, there's another story about Abraham preparing to sacrifice his beloved son Isaac. As Abraham began to plunge the knife into the heart of the thing he most loved in this world, God stayed his hand. God didn't really want what Abraham had been blessed with. He simply wanted Abraham to be very clear that there was something more valuable and worth the sacrifice.

I discovered the same about the money I had grown to value too highly. I had struggled with God for so long that afternoon, the back office had closed before I could submit my form. Before the market opened the next morning, a church officer called and said a mutual friend had suggested I help him with a substantial inheritance. And I tore up the form to invade God's principal in the retirement plan, as the business that had simply appeared had paid the month's mortgage.

Inspired by God's ability to provide for our true needs, within weeks I had given up the great view, the corporate title, the pension plan, and my own plans for my life. I moved my fledgling independent counseling firm into a spare bedroom in our home and listened as my wife home-schooled our young son nearby. As I heard Garrett learn to spell *c-a-t* and *d-o-g,* I developed a profound sense of what the sacrifice of an only son truly means. I never missed hearing my name called as the top producer in the office. I continued to grow reacquainted with the God of my youth. I fell in love with God, my family, my neighbors . . . and even myself once again. And it was all because God had never stopped loving me even as I worshiped at the altars of other religions.

———————————————

The Rev. Dr. Theodore Speers once said, "We have got to begin a vast reclamation project to revitalize religion for those to whom it means little or nothing. This can be done not by trying to persuade those outside the church to believe what we believe but by pointing out to them the presence of the unrecognized religion that already exists in their lives."[1] My experiences told me that he was prophetic. So in the past decade I've spent half my working time with people who need help with investments, and the other half with people who need help with the secular gods of American culture. And I have discovered what makes us modern Americans so skeptical of the God of Judeo-Christianity. It is paradox.

It makes no sense to most of my friends on Wall Street, but it seems the more time I spend with God and sharing his blessings with other people by writing, speaking, and just listening, the more people keep coming to me for investment advice. I am always careful to tell people that rather than seek me out, I'd rather they share my books and ideas with their counselors in the hope that they too might be enriched. But enough people keep coming that my family lives well and we have excess to share with others.

It is paradoxical to our marketing culture that I no longer advertise—but have new clients each month. It is paradoxical to those on the fast track that I don't even have a secretary after all these years—yet I still have plenty of time. But Jesus promised that if we'll seek first the kingdom of God, he'll add all the things we need. It is paradoxical to me even today, but he provides all the time I need to be with my family, write books, do radio commentary, serve on boards, speak at gatherings, and still earn a living as an investment advisor. In fact, one paradox I most appreciate about Jesus is that while he kept himself free from the pursuit of power and money, he has influenced and enriched billions of people, both Christian and non-Christian, in the two millennia since he walked this earth. The truth of that paradox could set many of us free for a more abundant life—one that begins today and extends throughout all eternity.

As God's thoughts are not our thoughts, Jesus had to be the Master of Paradox. He said, "The last will be first, and the first will be last" (Matt. 20:16). He added, "Whoever wants to be first must be slave of all" (Mark 10:44). Those thoughts make no sense to more rational types. Marx has sorely tempted liberal Americans with the idea that government elites can do our thinking about life for us. And Rand has sorely tempted libertarian Americans with the idea that our own thoughts about life are sufficient. While the ideas of Marx have been largely discredited, many of us, especially we business types, still have considerable faith in Rand's idea that simply pursuing money for ourselves can provide the good life here on earth.

But I'm more convinced today than ever that the paradoxical thoughts of Jesus Christ are the only way to a truly abundant life. For by humbly adopting the mind of Christ, I may not have found the utopian life that Marx and Rand promised here on earth, but I have found a saving faith in Christ that helps me deal with the realities of life—and death.

What have I been saved from? Many things—including many in this life. I have been saved from the confusion of mixing the thoughts of Christ with the thoughts of secular philosophers. This is a process that theologians call "syncretism" and that researcher George Barna calls "the preferred religion of Americans."

I have been saved from the futility of trying to figure out the complications of life solely with my own limited mind. I now have the revelations and experiences of the community of faith over the millennia to help me. And I've learned that a little mystery in life is an enriching thing, encouraging a sense of wonder and awe about life and God.

I—and my clients—have been saved from the idea that the government can provide true security through FDIC insurance, government securities, or Social Security.

We have been saved from the idea that government is sufficient in caring for our neighbors. So we are more ethical with our investments. It might surprise you, but my mentor and friend Sir John Templeton was the best-performing fund manager in the world over recent decades yet never financed companies primarily involved in casino gambling, tobacco, alcoholic beverages, and adult literature. It might also surprise you that women seem particularly interested in ethics. When the Lutheran Church recently asked their members which sex is most ethical, over fifty percent said women, while only ten percent said men. As Newt Gingrich said, it seems we men still like to run out of the cave and kill something.

Yet we have also been saved from the hatred of government that has kept my libertarian friends anxious and cynical about the prospect that our economy could strengthen and stocks could increase in value. So we have reaped a bountiful harvest as Americans are again thinking that the assets of the richest nation the world has ever known are indeed worth far more than we thought in the early '90s.

I and my clients have been saved from a pessimistic media that focuses on our $5 trillion federal debt while never giving thanks to God that our nation is blessed with $55 trillion worth of assets.

We have been saved from the futility of my trying to satisfy my former Wall Street superiors' demands for increasing revenues year in and year out.

I have been saved from thinking that my net worth is the measure of my success. So I have been saved from the treadmill to *Forbes* magazine's list of the four hundred richest people in America, a treadmill that I once confused with the ladder to heaven.

I have been saved from the illusion that the wealth of Bill Gates is more deserving of contemplation than the wealth of tens of millions of Christians who sit in our pews each week.

And I have been saved from the illusion that simply tithing, fasting, and praying in the temple, as the Pharisee did, can ever assure that I will see the political and economic realities of the world outside, as Jesus did. As he dearly appreciated, there is nothing so blinding as religious pride.

With the year 2000 upon us and so many Christian leaders warning about the end times, we may need to be saved from something else: false teaching about money and how we invest it. I am amazed at some of the advice being given by conservative Christians who believe the end is near, and even though I have been warned not to challenge that advice, I will respectfully, but emphatically, disagree with some of those leaders on these pages.

If you are looking for specific investment tips for those times, I won't disappoint you. But I hope you won't look ahead right away to see what they are. For this book, more than any I've written, is about biblical and spiritual principles. Before you can invest wisely with your heart, mind, and soul, you need to have very real answers to some very important questions.

What do you worship with your time, talent, and money? How does this affect your relationships with family, friends, and neighbors? Has this provided a truly abundant life or simple illusions of the good life? Are you noticing that life seems to be passing far more quickly than it used to? Are you truly investing for the days you have remaining here on earth and for all eternity?

In many ways, I've reconnected with the simple farm boy of my youth, only now I'm less interested in the American Dream and the American Capitol. By the world's standard I've finally made it. Like many of you, I'm wealthier than my parents, and I really don't need to worry about the wolf at my door. I do, however—and so do you—have to worry about a more devious intruder, one that could rob me not just of money but of my very soul. If the end, however we define it, is really near, it's time to take a much closer look at how to manage a little money without losing our souls.

Part One

HOW WE VIEW WEALTH

Many leaders, I'm afraid, place their religious and moral convictions in separate compartments and do not think of the implications of their faith on their responsibilities.

BILLY GRAHAM

We've put our concerns about morals and character "in a box," and prefer to worship at the altar of the economy. If the economy is all that matters, then we really are stupid.

CAL THOMAS

One

Looking at Money, Life, and Eternity

It is since Christians have ceased to think of the other world that they have become so ineffective in this. Aim at Heaven and you get earth "thrown in"; aim at earth and you will get neither.

C. S. LEWIS

It was early 1991. Iraq had just crossed the border into Kuwait, the Dow Jones Industrial Average had just crossed the 2500 level, and I had just appeared on a television show to discuss what the tensions in the Middle East might mean for the economy and investments.

When I got back to the office, my first call was from a pastor who had seen the show and needed investment counsel. Like most pastors, he wasn't overpaid. But he had inherited a fairly substantial amount of money that if reasonably invested might assure a few silver, if not golden, years for his wife and himself. If astutely invested, it would have allowed them to leave some money to their church and favorite ministries and charities.

The idea that he might ever possibly retire, much less produce enough extra wealth to endow religious and charitable work, had never entered his mind. Like most pastors I know, he was well versed in biblical concepts about sharing wealth but had missed the first financial lesson of the Bible, the one that says, "In the beginning God created . . . ." So I started at the beginning and explained that since we are created in the image of God, it's all right for us to create a little wealth to share with our families, churches, ministries, and charities. The trick is to do it without losing our souls to fear and/or greed—and without creating social problems that will essentially negate our future charitable activities. That is, the trick is to manage our wealth with spiritual and ethical principles.

He seemed intrigued as I began to explain the track records that a few prudent and ethical mutual funds had developed over decades. He was startled that one of my favorites, which was managed by a company that also managed money for several denominational pension plans, would have turned ten thousand dollars into over a million during the typical pastor's career. Though he was an independent pastor at a small church and not covered by any pension plan, he had just inherited a multiple of that ten thousand dollars. He had ample resources to give a little and invest a little for a much brighter future.

He reminded me of the children of Israel who, after a long, hard journey through the desert, were finally peering into the land of milk and honey. But like the Hebrews (and virtually every client I have counseled in twenty years), he too thought he saw an unconquerable giant looming in the Promised Land. In previous years the giants had been named Vietnam, OPEC, Watergate, a twenty-one percent prime rate, a Japan that was going to buy us, the federal debt, and so on. But this time the giant seemed to him as tall as Goliath. While most Americans would eventually name the conflict in the Middle East Desert Storm, he called it Armageddon.

Investment counselors throw a lot of stones at giants. Most of the time well-placed shots can bring them down to earth, where they can be beheaded. But this one proved that I was no David. The pastor explained that he might as well just leave his money in treasury bills, for "what does it matter where the money is invested if the world is about to end?"

As he hung up, I reflected once again that most of the Hebrews never saw a giant. Their simple *fear of encountering a giant* was enough to keep them wandering the desert rather than enjoying the land of milk and honey that God had promised for as long as anyone had listened. But as the quick victory in Desert Storm ignited the stock market to soar well over threefold during the years that followed, I realized that this was the first time that I had encountered anyone who used theology, as opposed to simple economic fear, to justify an unproductive investment. And I remembered that the ten spies who had cautioned the Hebrews about the unconquerable giants—and had thereby kept the Hebrews out of the Promised Land—had been very respected religious leaders. Yet they weren't God.

In subsequent years more and more conservative Christian clients seemed to talk more and more about Armageddon and economic earthquakes. The two seem to go together like bread and butter. And as the book of Revelation does put them together, the combination has influenced the worldview of Christians for millennia. But it could also be one of the signs of our times that we Christians are no longer sure what we should be worried about. While many of us have worried about the economic roof caving in due to an earthquake one day, the odds are better that the moral foundations of our country are being flooded away and its spiritual structure blown away as we have been distracted by far less likely events.

A lot of this looking for things in the future to worry about rather than dealing with the problems at hand has been due to our own media. As I listened to Christian radio, read Christian financial books, and watched Christian television during the early nineties, it was difficult to remember that Jesus once said in that famous sermon he delivered on the mount, "Do not worry, saying, 'What shall we eat?' or 'What shall we drink?' or 'What shall we wear?' For the pagans run after all these things, and your heavenly Father knows that you need them. But seek first his kingdom and his righteousness, and all these things will be given to you as well. Therefore do not worry about tomorrow, for tomorrow will worry about itself. Each day has enough trouble of its own" (Matt. 6:31–34). It's ironic that by that definition, many conservative Christians I've counseled in recent years have seemed very much like pagans. We always seem inclined to imagine in the future some economic giant that just can't be handled. And though our nation has not lost any battles to those giants, our modern equivalents of the ten spies have been enough to keep millions of us out of our own personal Promised Lands, both financially and spiritually.

A couple of radio stations provided an opportunity for me to debate those spies who had scouted the Promised Land and decided the giants were too big and fearsome for us to battle. The debate that essentially prompted this book took place in early 1995. It was with Don McAlvaney, an eternally pessimistic investment advisor and newsletter publisher who speaks often of Armageddon and is therefore widely quoted in end-times circles and on Christian radio.

I spent an hour in the debate, mostly listening as Don explained all the giants he imagined looming in the future. He recited the familiar litany that in coming weeks the debts of our nation were going to implode, America would be unable to compete with Third World countries, and so on. I simply explained why we should be most grateful that at the moment our nation was at peace and flowed with milk and honey, even if not the champagne wishes and caviar dreams of the rich and famous. I thought I was faring pretty well in refuting Don's vision that we stood "on the brink of one of the greatest financial disasters in history." But toward the end of the hour Don said I was "a good man" but I didn't "understand the times in which we live." He then quoted Proverbs 27:12, which says, "The prudent see danger and take refuge, but the simple keep going and suffer for it."

If there's a great commandment for Christians who diligently look for the giants in life, it is that verse. While I was hurt that Don thought I was simple (just kidding), I was more interested that it was the second time that I had heard theology, as opposed to simple economic fear, used to justify some rather unproductive investments. For when the host of the debate asked for specific portfolio suggestions, Don recommended that people completely avoid stocks, bonds, and real estate and instead divide their investments among treasury bills to protect against a collapsing stock market; gold coins to protect against a collapsing economy; and foreign currencies to protect against a collapsing dollar.

I simply asked Don how financing the federal debt by buying treasury bills (surprise! But that's what they do!), fearfully hoarding gold coins, and betting against our own currency was going to profit our children into the future. I then suggested it might be better stewardship to buy some stocks of the companies that might employ our children and to invest in bonds and CDs that finance the affordable housing that might shelter them. I acknowledged that might put some of God's resources prudently at risk, but it might also enrich our children, our nation, and our world.

Don didn't see things that way. He explained that our own democratically elected government—however imperfect, it is the last really big giant some of us have created in our own minds to keep us out of the Promised Land—had already stolen our children's future. He went on to explain that the best we could hope for was to protect what we have from the many slightly smaller giants he also saw in the immediate future. But of course all the anxiety and hoarding was done in the name of a Master who could reap where he did not sow. Presumably, this Master could also magically care for us and our children without us having to do anything but hoard what was entrusted to us. That of course was the terrible mistake of the third servant in the parable of the talents—the one who lost his soul by misinterpreting what the Master had expected.

And we should notice that the third servant of the parable also missed making a little money. For during the next three years after our debate the stock market soared from 4000 to 9000; gold dropped like the rock, however supposedly valuable, that it really was; the economy grew so quickly, even the doom-and-gloomers began to fear that the head of the Federal Reserve Board might tighten interest rates; and the dollar skyrocketed. And the people who bought into Don's investment plan were hurt even worse financially than the third servant, who at

least managed to break even. Also, the mental stress of expecting—
with the absolute certainty with which Don spoke—that one reality
was going to occur and watching as the exact opposite unfolded must
have caused great spiritual damage to many souls. And it could have
been prevented had we not put our faith in our government's securities,
gold coins, and the currencies of foreign nations rather than the perspective of Jesus, which encourages the productive use of our resources
for all rather than the fearful hoarding of resources for ourselves.

Yet not too surprisingly, after the stock market had soared,
unemployment had dropped to record lows, and the percentage of
Americans owning their own homes had risen to record highs,
some of the same ministries that had baptized the fear of the early
nineties began to see things differently. For example, Pat Robertson, who has recommended treasury bills to investors for most of
the nineties, has recently promoted a financial conference about
why everyone should be making "at least twenty percent in the
stock market this year and every year ... even without prior experience in the stock market."[1]

I found that intriguing, as my friend and mentor Sir John M.
Templeton was apparently the most successful mutual fund manager in the world over the past five decades by averaging fifteen percent per year. Even that is an amazing record when you consider
that the stocks of America's largest companies have averaged a little
over ten percent per year during the past seven decades. So twenty
percent each and every year would be quite a stretch, even if Sir
John wasn't now saying the recent run-up makes it more likely than
not that we're vulnerable to a forty percent or more drop over the
next five years. So despite the Bible's teaching that the love of
money is the root of at least as much mischief as is fear, it seems
some of our church leaders are now content to baptize the greed
that has recently captured the hearts and minds of our culture.

Financially, switching from fear to greed as our culture does
may be even more dangerous to your financial health than the
advice offered by persistent pessimists. While the paranoids do both

financial and spiritual harm by keeping us fearfully hoarding gold coins and such, the mere pessimists often do relatively little financial harm by keeping us in government bonds and certificates of deposit, though the spiritual harm they cause remains considerable. Yet those who have fluctuated between fear and greed have hurt us much worse. They often keep us out of stocks when stocks are low, due to fear. But they put us into stocks when stocks are high, due to greed. And it's most difficult to prosper when you buy when prices are high and sell when they are lower.

Due to such mischief, I now spend considerable time helping people understand how the fear-and-greed theologies of humans can be in such conflict with the prudent and charitable teachings of God. In Don's case I believe it is a rather simple misunderstanding of Scripture and how we should use it in all its fullness rather than parts of it for our own purposes. The proverb he quoted says the prudent *see* danger. It does not say they *imagine* danger in the future. As we approach the year 2000, differentiating between the two could be most instrumental in helping you make a little money without losing your soul. Just remember that Ecclesiastes 8:7 says, "Since no man knows the future, who can tell him what is to come?"

I will leave it up to the theologians to determine if God, who does know the future, still speaks through prophets or not. But I render my opinion that if God still does, he has little interest in predicting the U.S. stock market or the price of gold coins. So we should be prudent at all times. And we should even be fearful on rare occasions.

In a Golden Nugget

You will be a more productive and therefore rewarded servant if you don't attempt to play Master.

If you open your front door and see a grizzly bear, fear is a wonderful gift of God. But if you're always afraid to open your front door because you imagine a grizzly bear will be behind it, the fear is not of God and you are not being prudent.

In a golden nugget, which is my way of saying this is a particularly enriching point, you will be a more productive and therefore rewarded servant if you don't attempt to play Master. And as we approach the year 2000, that will be a lot easier if you compare the visions of self-anointed economic prophets with how Jesus taught us to look at things.

At this point you may be tempted to think, as Don did, that I'm simply a Pollyannaish optimist who got lucky as the stock market soared in the early nineties. You should know how I see things at the moment. As I edit this book in the summer of 1998, the Dow Jones Industrial Average is near the 9000 level. I can *see* that it is very high by historic standards. (There will be greater details on that later.) I don't know what it is going to do. And lots of people are now imagining that it can only go higher in the future. But I've been taking profits in my blue-chip stocks and am content to let others speculate on the future. If you'll forgive a bad pun, there may indeed be a bear market knocking as I write. Perhaps not. I'm simply employing the resources I steward in areas where I can see there are greater values—and greater needs for God's resources—than exist in the U.S. stock market at this time. We'll get to those later as well, when you have a better perspective of how to use them.

Americans have now enjoyed seven fat years since the lean ones of the last recession. That is one of the longest economic expansions in memory. While a growing number of very human economists are now telling us that the business cycle has been repealed, a biblical perspective tells me the odds are good that we are due some of those lean years that the world has experienced since the days of Joseph.

At the very least, stock markets tend to take two steps forward and one step back. And those movements aren't always in lockstep with the economy. (Do you remember that the crash of 1987 wasn't accompanied by a recession?) As the Dow Jones Industrial Average has soared from the 2000 level to the 9000 level during this decade, a correction to even the 5500 level would not be all that unusual. During this century we have experienced market declines of forty percent or more once every nine years on average. We haven't seen such a decline since the early seventies. Yet one of a similar nature might still leave us far above the 3000 level, where some doom-and-gloomers I debated in the early nineties advised us to bail out. And if history is still a reliable indicator—and I expect it is a fairly useful one—the market should be far higher than today's levels in coming decades. In fact, I'm now working on a newspaper article about why it may see the 1,000,000 level during the next century, assuming there is one. (Strange as it may seem, that only requires compounding at a five percent annual rate.)

Clearly notice that I'm not predicting a decline in the immediate future. I'm only pointing out that a normal recession, a normal stock market correction, and the year 2000 will make the doomsters very confident once again. And they could prove right this time. That is one reason why I try to live each day as though the world might end tomorrow, just as it might on January 1, 2000— or to be more precise, January 1, 2001, the true beginning of the new millennium. And a stopped clock is precisely right twice a day. That makes it more accurate, if far less useful, than the many running clocks that are off ever so slightly. So sooner or later we may experience what the doomsters have been predicting for decades. And the world will rush to proclaim them modern prophets. I only hope they haven't kept you from planting and harvesting during the past seven fat years because God wasn't quite as clear with them about his timing for the seven lean years as he was with Joseph.

Eschatology: The End of the Age(s)

While reflecting on the end of things for these several months, I've grown to believe that Jesus taught at least three eschatologies.

The first was a personal eschatology. When he said, "The kingdom of God is within you" (Luke 17:21), Jesus may have been referring to the spiritual transformation of the human heart, soul, and mind, or the end of our own individual pagan age. This is what many evangelicals call being "born again" and Baptists call "beginning a personal

relationship with Jesus Christ." The second was an ethical eschatology. When Jesus said, "The kingdom of heaven is near" (Matt. 4:17),
he may have been saying that these new children of God would
begin to change our world by feeding the poor, comforting the
afflicted, and so on. This is the social ministry that appeals to mainline and Catholic Christianity. And the third was an apocalyptic
eschatology, or the end of history that preoccupies many fundamentalist Christians. This was when Jesus spoke of the sheep and
goats, or the great judgment, and told the sheep, "Come, take your
inheritance, the kingdom prepared for you since the creation of the
world" (Matt. 25:34).

Theologians sometimes explain these three eschatologies—which
greatly influence the way we live our Christianity—by comparing
them to a train ride. Speaking very generally, many evangelicals and
Baptists are primarily focused on encouraging others to get on the
right train. Mainline Christians and Catholics often focus more on
making the ride through life more comfortable. And fundamentalists
are more focused on what happens beyond the station at the end
of the line.

In my view, each is correct but less than the fullness that Jesus taught.
It is therefore the goal of this book to explore all three eschatologies.
However, it is also my view that most of us American Christians want
to get on the right train, and absolutely everyone wants to arrive at
the proper destination. Yet many want to simply enjoy the ride in
between. Therefore this book is primarily focused on the work that
needs to be accomplished to keep the train on track.

Let's think a little more about the pastor's end-times theology,
in which it doesn't matter where in the world we invest because the
world's coming to an end anyway. For we need to contrast that with
Jesus' teaching that where we invest makes all the difference in an
eternity that's just beginning. I've concluded that the real problem

with end-times theology, at least as the pastor and many others seem to understand it, is that it is only concerned with the end of this world, sort of a religious secularism. As ironic as it may seem, being preoccupied with the end of this world left the pastor no time to reflect on how his stewardship will be judged in the next. And as C. S. Lewis observed, when we Christians cease to think of the next world, we become most ineffective in this . . . and gain neither this world nor the next.

So the year 2000 may be arriving at just the right moment. I know very few people who would argue that the American church is an effective force in the world at the moment, especially in how it deals with the "Big Three" temptations of money, sex, and power. If the year 2000 prompts Americans, especially the baby boomers beginning their spiritual quests, to again think of the next world, *as opposed to the simple end of this one,* a much needed Second Reformation just might occur. And that would enrich us in ways we can hardly imagine.

It's interesting to reflect that it was a preacher named Tetzel's poor stewardship theology that ignited Martin Luther's passion and launched the first Reformation in the sixteenth century. Tetzel, of course, was a fund-raiser for the medieval Catholic Church. The stewardship perspective he spread was that a soul could be saved if the faithful would simply give a few coins to a church that had grown increasingly irrelevant and self-serving. His lack of concern for those who provided the coins literally prompted Luther to tack his ninety-five suggestions about true religion on the door of Wittenberg Church. Perhaps the equally poor stewardship theologies of recent years could ignite our passions, launch the Second Reformation, and again make the church a guiding light before a money culture wandering in a spiritual desert. If so, the questionable financial perspectives of Christianity in recent years might again be a wonderful case of God working in strange ways.

Yet there are many dangers—to both the health of your personal finances and the health of the church—to be avoided as we deal with the year 2000. End-times books, articles, and talks are proliferating. As I have begun to read and hear various people discussing wealth and the ultimate nature of things, they seem to look at it from various perspectives. These perspectives appear in the remaining chapters of this book. Not all of them are biblical, spiritual, or traditionally Christian. Clearly notice that those that most often keep us from making money without losing our souls always seem too small in one way or another. Some are rational but void of heart and soul, some are emotional but void of thought and the eternal dimension, some are purely humanistic rather than also godly, some are purely secular rather than also spiritual, and so on. If we are truly created in the image of God and expect God's blessings on our financial activities, we should see things more as God does, from the larger, more complete perspective.

Of particular concern to us here, over the past two decades I've learned that many authors, television ministers, and investment advisors prosper by affirming what people already *feel*. In other words, in money matters we tend to be highly emotional rather than rational and spiritual. Few Americans *know* many, if any, facts about the economy. For example, as you *felt* that America was going broke in the early nineties, did you ever hear the value of America's assets discussed as authors, ministers, and brokers repeatedly told you about the size of the federal debt? When such emotional perspectives fill people's hearts with fear, gloomy books hit the best-seller lists, contributions pour in to conservative ministries and politicians who want to reduce government spending, and gold coins sell very well. Then as our culture gradually *feels* better about the federal debt, the stock market soars, people's *feelings* turn to greed, prosperity books are all the rage, ministries hold seminars on the stock market, and speculative investment strategies prosper those who market them.

On the other side of the coin, I've learned that readers, listeners, and investors prosper by looking beyond the conventional wisdom being preached and sold at the moment. If you planted when things looked cloudy in the early nineties and are reaping as the skies have cleared, you had to avoid the cultural religion shaped by authors, brokers, and ministers. That's something true religion has helped us do since Moses had the good sense not to conduct an opinion poll about the Ten Commandments. (The first tension between true religion and a cultural religion that people wanted is described in Exodus 32 and occurred when Moses came down from the mount and Aaron described the development of the golden calf.) And it was a politician, not a moral leader, who asked the people to vote for either Jesus or Barabbas (Matt. 27:17).

In a Golden Nugget

In God's political economy the customer or the voter is not always right.

In a golden nugget, in God's political economy the customer or the voter is not always right.

Our marketing-oriented culture assures that you may have trouble looking at financial matters as Jesus did, at least at first. And if the past decade of my life is any indication, he's about to upset some tables in that temple you call your financial perspective. The *true* theology of Jesus has never been all that popular with people, as it insists we must be vulnerable to many thorns and crosses in life. So even we religious leaders are often tempted to create more popular, self-protecting ways of looking at things. As we are most human, we like to be popular, like to fill churches, and even like to sell lots of books. As an author, I confess this is the first book in which I've simply said what I think needs to be said rather than what the institutional church and its members might want to hear.

As an investment advisor, I know only too well that Christian financial planners can endear themselves to both wealthy investors and religious institutions alike by teaching we're super-Christians if we simply tithe ten percent of our excess wealth ... even if Jesus didn't teach any such thing. As a conservative media commentator who often talks about political economy, I know I can endear myself to my listeners and readers by teaching we shouldn't pay taxes to that "Babylon" we now call Washington ... even if Jesus didn't teach that either. The opportunities for astute marketing to your way of looking at things go on and on. But they will do little to help you make a little money without losing your soul. If we are to receive God's richest blessings, we must look at things as Jesus taught us to.

Jesus looked at money and the ultimate rewards of life in very simple, integrated, and wise ways. Our secular culture likes to complicate, compartmentalize, and confuse the way it seeks temporary rewards. And Jesus' hostile encounters with religious authorities attest that there are few surer ways of obscuring the material and spiritual riches of God than with the theologies of humans. If Jesus' teaching about being "born again" has a financial dimension—and I believe it does—it means you need to begin the painful experience of forgetting almost everything you have been taught about money by both the world and the church, for they are much the same thing. Most of us aren't born fearing economic earthquakes or born greedy enough to want to be in the *Forbes* list of the four hundred richest people in America. We are too often taught fear and greed by those of the media, those of power, and those of the cloth. I will try to help Jesus unteach both fear and greed.

If I do my job properly in the first part of this book, the financial perspective of Jesus will give you a new worldview, will dramatically rearrange your current thinking, and will then restructure your financial plan. You can't seriously listen to Jesus talk about money without undergoing what our world might call a "radical paradigm shift" or what Saint Paul called a "renewing of your mind" (Rom. 12:2). After a decade of trying it myself and with clients, I know very well that this is every bit as painful as the birth experience. As we proceed, you will discover just how conditioned we are to look at life from the "Enlightenment" perspective, which is often confused with the Christian perspective. So my job is to challenge you as far out of your comfort zone about money as possible, not so you might make even more money but so you might not lose your soul, which is far more valuable.

Finally, your new worldview and new way of thinking must be put into action. If you simply think and see the world as Jesus did and don't live your faith, I have made a very bad stewardship decision. I will have completely wasted my time, talent, and treasure as well as your time. I will have simply created one more illusion in this old world by having you think you live as a Christian when you don't. And you will experience *even greater tension* over money than most Americans do today, as they're most at peace with their god.

It's tempting to tell you that you can pursue the riches we Americans do and still expect a smooth journey to profound peace with Jesus. But that would deny Jesus' own teaching about the eye of the needle (Matt. 19:24). If we're to be serious about Jesus and money, let us honestly admit now that we face a difficult struggle. Paradoxically, there's a certain peace in that honesty. For it is only the serious understanding of that truth, rather than the denial of its reality, that may allow us to gain the world without losing our souls.

As we anxiously but hopefully anticipate the year 2000, we are surrounded by a lot of differing perspectives, most of them secular and humanistic. Yet there will never be a better time to see things more clearly by looking at things the way Jesus did. For no matter what we read, hear, think, and feel about the year 2000, it is certain that the time granted for each of us to journey on this earth *is* coming to an end. And our conversation with the Master about how we've chosen to invest his resources will become a very personal one—one that will assure returns, whether positive or negative, that even the most gifted investment analyst would find impossible to calculate.

TWO

A Personal View: Twenty Enriching Years of Looking at Money

What we see as we go through life always depends upon where we stand to look. Many a man who tries to talk as if he were standing on a mountain, shows by what he says that he is up to his eyes in the mud.

BILLY SUNDAY

In two decades of investment counseling, writing, and doing commentary, one of the most important things I've learned is that the perspectives of people are at least as important, and probably far more important, than the facts of matters. For example, few of us would argue with the fact that the sun rose this morning. Yet from a scientific perspective, the sun did absolutely nothing. The earth rotated. It simply doesn't seem so from our rather limited and rather self-centered perspectives. And our perspectives are typically shaped by our religious training, our education, our culture, and our personal experiences, particularly our painful experiences.

The same principle applies to making money without losing your soul. As you now know, I have often debated pessimists who have been enormously concerned with the federal debt. As it is the most recent of life's problems that got out of proper perspective, I'll use it occasionally throughout this book to clarify how a true Christian perspective can bless us.

The more sophisticated economic literature has been quite clear for years that the federal debt wasn't nearly the giant some of us imagined. For example, the *Economist* magazine has said, "The simple conclusion that a generation which inherits a national debt of, say, fifty percent of GDP [gross domestic product, or national income] is bound to be better off than one which inherits a national debt of, say, one hundred percent is confused—and often wrong. This is because the thinking that likens a national debt to an individual's debt is itself largely fallacious."[1] That perspective will become clearer as you read on. But for now simply understand that things got out of perspective as we looked at them from our small view as individuals dealing with our own personal debts rather than as a nation dealing with the march of history.

And while some of the pessimists I have encountered have painfully experienced the personal bondage of debt, most have also looked at it from their personal political perspectives as libertarians. That perspective sees government as the root of all evil and therefore believes few blessings can occur as long as it exists. As I listen to tapes of my debates with those of that perspective, I am always amazed at how they essentially ignored the facts about our economy, even as I read statistics from the most reliable *private* sources, and relied solely on their cynical perspective of government. That's rather strange, as government at all levels only affects about one-third of our economy through taxing and spending. So it's doubtful government should dominate their worldview. And that perspective has done little to help them make a little money without losing their souls, for the economy was doing fine as they anxiously worried over the debt.

The same may prove true of the new perspective that stocks can only go up. The facts about the stock market indicate valuations have never been so high. Yet few of my clients now care much for those facts, due to their current perspective. Studies tell us that over ninety percent of the money now in the stock market was invested after the crash of 1987 and that one-half of Americans who now own stocks didn't own any in 1990. So this perspective is obviously a new one. But despite the facts about the stock market's high valuations, the new optimistic perspective is now held to as devoutly as the old pessimistic perspective was only a few short years ago.

All this is rather un-Christian. The Christian perspective has always been that truth often resides outside our own human hearts and minds. We therefore invite Jesus into our hearts, as our own feelings of fear and greed can distort our worldviews and cost us dearly. (The liturgical churches have historically prayed, "Incline our hearts to keep this law." There would be no need for God's help if our hearts naturally embraced such law.) And we study the Holy Scriptures to let in the revelations of God, as the thinking in our own minds is far too limited for true success. Finally, Jesus asked us to "look at the birds of the air" (Matt. 6:26), as there are truths to be learned around us. But modern humanism—with its proclamation that the human heart is good and the human mind is sufficient—has largely closed us off from any truth outside ourselves. So we close off any economic statistics that may not agree with our own feelings and thinking. And that rarely leads to making a little money without losing our souls.

So while my previous books have focused on the facts concerning the economy and investing, this one will be primarily concerned with perspective, especially the Christian perspective. I believe Jesus was absolutely correct when he said his way will produce a more abundant life than will the several other ways that surround us. For example, the Christian perspective has traditionally been more influenced by the thirteenth chapter of Romans than by libertarian political philosophies. Though written as the barbarous Nero ruled, that chapter encourages a perspective of honor and respect for government and says we have nothing to fear from it, assuming we behave ourselves. That perspective could have enriched millions of us in recent years. So might the Christian perspective that, regardless of Wall Street's and some ministers' view, greed is *not* good and we should have few expectations that stocks will produce returns twice the historic norm year in and year out. And both Christian perspectives concerning fear and greed might validate the old saying that we're often punished *by* our sins in this life rather than simply *for* our sins in the next.

———————————————

As we explore the various ways you can look at life, money, and eternity, you should know how my perspective pales when compared with God's. I begin with a confession: After fifty years in our churches, twenty years on Wall Street, and ten years of considerable soul-searching, I've never been able to determine exactly what the parable of the talents means. When I was with a major Wall Street firm, I took pride in identifying with the first servant, who after all did earn more than twice as much as even the second servant. After I established my own firm to help the few religious and ethical investors I knew who truly wanted their money where their beliefs were, my far smaller client list helped me to identify with the second servant. He made half the money the first servant did— but earned identical rewards for eternity from the master anyway.

I used to help people who had a little more—and sometimes a lot more—money than they knew what to do with make even more. That's a pretty good definition of an investment counselor, at least as it's understood in our money culture. But I've grown to agree with Andrew Carnegie that "millionaires who laugh are rare, very rare indeed," and I am now trying to see my client's needs from a different perspective.

I don't know how much I should do for the poor and how much I should do for my family and myself. After all, Jesus never commanded us to love our neighbors *instead of* ourselves. After ten years of wrestling with God over that balance, the ideal of Jesus to "sell everything you have and give to the poor" (Mark 10:21) still frightens me to the depths of my soul. The teaching of John the Baptist that "the man with two tunics should share with him who has none" (Luke 3:11) fills me with nearly as much anxiety. I take hope in the fact that if Jesus ever told Nicodemus, Joseph of Arimathea, or others to do either, it is not recorded in the Scriptures. And I find comfort in the teaching of C. S. Lewis, who said,

> I do not believe one can settle how much we ought to give. I am afraid the only safe rule is to give more than we can spare. In other words, if our expenditure on comforts, luxuries, amusements, etc., is up to the standard common among those with the same income as our own, we are probably giving too little. If our charities do not at all pinch or hamper us, I should say that they are too small. There ought to be things we should like to do and cannot do because our charitable expenditure excludes them.[2]

I suffer no delusions of being a financial saint. I find it quite difficult enough just being a struggling disciple. And having witnessed the hubris that often drives many of us to think we can write and speak authoritatively not only about religion but also about politics and money, I often reflect on these words from Thomas Merton:

> And now I am thinking of the disease which is spiritual pride. I am thinking of the peculiar unreality that gets into the hearts of the saints and eats their sanctity away before it is mature. There is something of this worm in the hearts of all religious men ... The pleasure that is in his heart when he does difficult things and succeeds in doing them well, tells him secretly, "I am a saint." ... When someone opposes his desires he folds his hands humbly and seems to accept it for the time being, but in his heart he is saying: "I am persecuted by worldly men. They are incapable of understanding one who is led by the Spirit of God. With the saints it has always been so." Having become a martyr, he is ten times as stubborn as before.[3]

Nor do I intend to make a saint out of you. One of my dearest beliefs is that the world needs tens of millions of struggling disciples doing just a little more for the kingdom far more than it needs another saint or two for us to admire from a distance. So I simply invite people to join me as another disciple in that famous struggle through the eye of the needle. While I believe Jesus when he says that journey is possible "with God" (Mark 10:27), the difficulty of the journey reminds me that François Fénelon once wrote, "Chains of gold are no less chains than those of iron."[4]

For me, the journey has always been one not toward perfection but toward balance in life. After decades of hard work and saving, my family lives in one of those gated golf course communities that Florida is so famous for, but we live in the least expensive home in the community. They tell me I can afford a bigger home on my income, but staying where we are allows us to give a little more. We drive two cars that are considered premium makes, but we purchased them slightly used and they now have almost three hundred thousand miles on them. My wife probably needs a newer model, but she treasures the thank-you notes we get from those who do not even dream of owning cars and is determined to drive her old one until it "returns to the dust from whence it came!"

My wife and I work out of our home and don't even have a secretary, something our Wall Street friends can't imagine, but we've watched our son grow up, something our parents couldn't always do and our friends can't imagine either. By the world's standards, even if not by Wall Street's, we still make a wonderful living, but we are now free to spend half our time helping to shape the kingdom.

I am always tempted to make new commitments to my work each week, but I know Jesus was a person who kept himself free for others, and I'm trying to be more like him.

I'm a fairly logical person, but I now better appreciate the paradoxes of faith. For example, only spending half my time on purely financial matters doesn't inspire confidence among many potential clients. Yet my existing clients have grown to appreciate it. I spent around eighteen hours a day during the eighties looking for new investment opportunities. And I always found lots of them. That meant lots of trading, with its attendant costs and taxes. Many investors do much the same today, often at the encouragement of those selling investment advice and investment services. Yet the most successful investors that I have taken the time to study in recent years take a far different approach.

Peter Lynch, the legendary former manager of the Fidelity Magellan Fund, often says that if investors spend fifteen seconds a year thinking about the economy, they have probably wasted ten seconds. That's his way of saying that no one knows what it will do and that it doesn't matter, as good investments are always to be found. Legendary investor Warren Buffett says the key to investing is to simply buy a few quality investments and hold on long enough for them to go up, rather than frantically trade new ideas when each new issue of various publications arrives. And my mentor and friend Sir John Templeton has long devoted half his time to religious matters. He too says that he has never known what the economy or stocks will do but that it makes no difference. In fact, he says he was never as successful at investing until he moved to the Bahamas and was no longer influenced by the financial media. Yet his Templeton Growth Fund would have turned ten thousand dollars into over three million during the past half century. That is apparently the best performance of any mutual fund in the world. I haven't met too many investors who have done better than that by being preoccupied with economics and short-term trading.

My point is that an eternal perspective in how we should handle money is far more important than the monthly decisions most of us make in the way we invest our money.

I am interested in politics, but I don't believe it is the way to salvation. I've long been a Republican, but I don't equate that with being a Christian. I don't believe Jesus ever encouraged government welfare for the poor; if I did, I would probably be known as a "limousine liberal" or one of those who live in luxury while expecting the government to care for the poor. I do believe that Jesus taught we all are free to arrange our finances so we may love our neighbors as ourselves, an idea central to us who Robert Schuller of the Crystal

Cathedral has dubbed "Christian capitalists." Limousine liberals sometimes judge our Christian capitalist ideas harshly. I'm sure we can live with that. I only pray that God is more graceful and that the liberals might one day look at things as Mother Teresa did when she said, "We have no right to judge the rich. For our part, what we desire is not a class struggle but a class encounter, in which the rich save the poor and the poor save the rich."[5]

Nor do I suffer any delusions of being a financial prophet. Again, I often reflect on the insight of Thomas Merton, who said, "It is a terrible thing when one gets the idea he is a prophet or a messenger of God or a man with a mission to reform the world. . . . He is capable of destroying religion and making the name of God odious to men."[6] So I try to be a simple student who is privileged to climb the financial mountain occasionally, listen both to God and to disciples who may have a higher view of our modern world, and bring their insights back down for friends who are too busy with life in the valley to make the climb themselves. If that doesn't always produce the idealistic perspective of Jesus, I hope it occasionally produces the thought-provoking perspective of C. S. Lewis.

While I am the kind of person you might therefore expect to be preoccupied with finding a proper balance between money, politics, and religion, I am not the kind you might expect to be remotely interested in looking at the end times. Yet I am devoting considerable time, talent, and treasure to the subject, for both you and myself. My own spiritual life will be enriched if I reflect on eternity for a while. Yet the missed financial opportunities and spiritual damage caused by the experiences I described in the introduction are the primary reason for this particular stewardship decision.

I once shared a tape of my and Don McAlvaney's 1995 debate with a friend. He is a serious Christian who often hurt his spirit and finances by listening to pessimistic Christian financial advisors a few years ago. (Yet ironically, when I recently told him I am now exchanging some of my blue-chip stocks for other investments, he spent almost five minutes telling me why the economy can't stop

growing and why blue-chip stocks can't stop going up!) So I
expected him to agree with the optimistic point of view I had
expounded during the debate. But he agreed with Don, who had
said repeatedly that if I was right and the markets continued higher,
people would make a little more money, but if he, Don, was right
about the markets crashing and people took my advice, they would
lose it all and then some.

I've never been able to figure out why many Americans
assumed during the early nineties that gold coins, treasury securities, and foreign currencies couldn't lose purchasing power and that
stocks, bonds, and real estate couldn't gain it. Decades of experience had told us the exact opposite. It may be human nature to see
greener grass on the other side of the fence, but it was a peculiarly
American tendency in those years for some of us to see the grass
on our side of the fence as parched. And it was peculiarly American
for Christians to count problems rather than blessings. So while
Don and others had us hoarding gold coins and worrying about an
economic earthquake during the early nineties, the other nations I
visited were envious of our economy, were buying our stocks and
bonds, and were hoarding our currency. Apparently, they saw
things more clearly than we did.

Yet it was at that very moment that I realized that *no power on
earth*—such as the desire for material riches that motivates so many
of my friends on Wall Street—can get some people to look beyond
their self-interest and practice faithful stewardship. And no power
on earth can get fearful people to willingly encounter the giants in
our future. They need far greater rewards, and a cosmic Power, to
take the risks that the faithful stewards from the parable of the talents did. That we have such a Power is what Caleb and Joshua tried
to tell the Hebrews in the thirteenth and fourteenth chapters of
Numbers. And Jesus used some of his precious time on earth to tell
us that the abundant life requires that stewardship be kept in the
context of eternal riches. So one has to wonder: as central as those
old stories from our youth are to Judeo-Christianity, why have we

heard so very little of them lately and desperately need to hear them again, with the open minds and hearts of little children?

————————————

Until very recently, I've been a conservative Episcopalian since I married. But I grew up in a tiny, rural, and very conservative Southern Baptist church. We used to grow tobacco from Monday to Saturday and talk about the evils of alcohol on Sunday. (Now many Episcopalians I know drink from Monday to Saturday and talk about the evils of tobacco on Sunday!) I used to hide when I experimented with the hand-rolled product of our labors, as I knew my father would tan me if he caught me smoking. My high school basketball coach was also my health teacher. In health class he would explain how bad smoking was for us. After school he would threaten that if he caught us smoking, he'd kick us off the basketball team—something akin to excommunication in Kentucky. But when practice was finished, he would often recruit some of us to help him harvest his tobacco crop. So I've always known that the ethics of Christian economics are rather "nuanced" in modern America.

Yet the understanding of that nuance, which is the compartmentalization we detest in politicians, is one aspect of my moral education that was gathered from the "informal" sector. I recall a pastor from my high school years telling me privately that if he weren't a minister, he couldn't seek employment in the tobacco industry, as he wasn't sure about its morality. Despite my youth, I noticed I had never heard that way of looking at things preached from our pulpit. That's not to entirely blame the minister. He was a good man and a good friend to me. But had he attempted to share his perspective of Christian economics, I expect he would have been preaching to "half a choir" the next week.

But a few businesspeople sense that the controversy has theological dimensions. *Forbes* magazine has observed, "An interesting theological discovery has emerged from the battle over the federal budget: The cigarette manufacturers can buy indulgence for their sins by handing over a large sum of money to Washington. Of course, the money generated by any proposed increased levy on cigarettes must ultimately come from smokers which means that . . . it will come disproportionately from lower income earners."[7] But how many of us Christians see that issue theologically or understand that it involves the poor whom Jesus loved so dearly?

Though we were serious people of the Book when I was growing up, I don't think we were fundamentalists. Even if we were, I wouldn't consider fundamentalism the horrible thing my more thoughtful Christian friends seem to today. In fact, I might even recommend the approach from time to time. As we're a sports-oriented culture, let me use a sports metaphor to explain. I played a lot of golf when I was in the army. Whenever my game got off track, I would go back to a simple book by Ben Hogan entitled *The Modern Fundamentals of Golf.* It is one of the all-time classics about the game, and I still keep it on my desk, right beside my Bible and three other classics that keep me on track in other areas of life. I know it can't produce the touch and rhythm that hours of disciplined practice and play can. But when things go wrong with my swing, it is usually due to my forgetting a very fundamental principle. The same is true of religious life. I've spent many hours reading religious views in recent years. When we've gone wrong, it has usually been because we have forgotten a very fundamental principle, such as the commandment to love our neighbors, even our enemies, as ourselves.

The same principle applies to money, life, and eternity. Though the parable of the talents is a very fundamental teaching, I do not remember any sermons or classes during my youth concerning the end times, much less how they related to money. Perhaps that's because we had no money to relate to. But just to be sure that I wasn't distracted by the bugs, frogs, and other diversions that often kept me from listening to the ministers, I've checked with my mother to see if I might have missed anything. She doesn't remember any teaching about the end times, either. I consider that authoritative, as she rarely misses a word from any minister.

So for me, the apocalyptic passages from Daniel and Revelation have always been obscured by the Ten Commandments and the Sermon on the Mount. That's not a totally bad thing. But it would seem that during the five or six years that Mom and Dad once took me to church without missing a Sunday, I would have heard *something* about the setting of the stage on which my soul will be judged for all eternity ... and especially about how the clutter of our money culture might trip me up once I'm on that stage.

The same phenomenon continued during my formal education. I received a degree in political science at the University of Kentucky. The idea that the Puritans founded our country to be a "city on a hill" (Matt. 5:14), built it on a Protestant work ethic, and maintained it with a Calvinist sense of self-denial was given very little consideration. Yet this idea could be most useful today.

Perhaps you've heard that a Calvinist is one who believes it's all right to make money as long as he doesn't enjoy it? If not, you'll better appreciate, and perhaps kid, your Presbyterian and Reformed friends if you remember the insight, though the Reformed guys have learned to enjoy money more than they once did. Yet it is important to note, as the Calvinists did, that the faithful servants from the parable of the talents never spent all their earnings on themselves. The *Economist* magazine recently ran an article entitled "The Sorry State of Saving." It said, "Last year Americans put only 4.3 percent of their disposable income in the piggy bank, just about half as much as their parents salted away in 1967. Unless this trend toward profligacy is stemmed, and preferably reversed, America's 'miracle economy' will rest on shaky foundations. Less obvious, however, is how to do it."[8]

Perhaps a little Calvinist self-denial delivered by the church to balance the promotions delivered by television from Madison Avenue would be an enriching thing after all. Yet as I contemplated seminary in the late eighties, I discovered that seminaries rarely teach *anything* concerning the moral foundations of political economy and personal financial management, although that was a favorite topic of Moses and Jesus. Even George Bernard Shaw believed that "whether you think Jesus was God or not, you must admit that he was a first-rate political economist."[9] I know very few pastors today who could preach a really good sermon on Mr. Shaw's conviction, and he wasn't known for being a really good Christian.

If recent history is any indication, most attempts by pastors to preach such a sermon might sound remarkably similar to a mailing from a political action committee, though Jesus stayed above such approaches. So I would encourage us to begin with Russian author and dissident Aleksandr Solzhenitsyn's perspective:

> In my most evil moments I was convinced that I was doing good. And it was only when I lay there on rotting prison straw that I sensed within myself the first stirrings of good. Gradually it was disclosed to me that the line separating good and evil passes not through states, not between classes, nor between political parties either—but right through every human heart—and through all human hearts.... Since then I have come to understand the truth of all the religions of the world: They struggle with the evil inside a human being (inside every human being). It is impossible to expel evil from the world in its entirety, but it is possible to constrict it within each person.[10]

That's why Jesus fled when the people tried to make him a king. It is paradoxical, but focusing on the human heart rather than politics and money made Jesus the "first-rate political economist" that Shaw so greatly appreciated. Perhaps the same perspective could make modern Americans equally appreciative of Jesus. If so, the church as an institution may need to change the way it looks at things.

After I decided not to pursue seminary, I tried for years to use whatever gifts God has given me to help in the work of my Episcopal Church. For years I went to "stewardship" conferences. Each one was a group of lawyers talking about how to create charitable trusts, or ordained ministers talking about how to get the annual pledge cards in. Either way, it seemed stewardship was simply about fund-raising. After years of such meetings, one national leader finally asked those attending the meeting what might interest them. The number one response was "socially responsible investing." As I had written one of the only books on the subject from a Christian perspective, I assured the leader I hadn't encouraged their response. He said he just had to have me speak. But the next year, we listened to three attorneys talk about how to create charitable remainder trusts.

About the same time, the *Wall Street Journal* conducted a survey of some of the best-known "Christian financial planners" around America. It concluded that with the exception of their recommending that clients give to ministries rather than secular charities, it couldn't see that the Christian financial planners did anything different with money than their secular counterparts.[11]

Those examples are a metaphor for the relationship between wealth and the church today. Interestingly, a more recent *Wall Street Journal* article said that "the relationship between wealth and religion is becoming a hot topic"[12] in financial seminars, books, and so on. Unfortunately, the article went on to say that most people get their perspective from outside the church, turning primarily to New Age leaders. In short, many Americans are devoting considerable time and money to understanding the spiritual and moral dimensions of money, but the church keeps talking about fund-raising.

I never went to another stewardship conference for my denomination. But I did begin to teach denominational stewardship leaders who had gathered in national conferences. And after several years of doing so, my pastor asked for another chance to figure out how to use my gifts within the local church. I very reluctantly agreed to try one more time. But after a joint meeting with our bishop, we agreed that the only thing I could do was to keep coming on Sunday morning and giving when they passed the plate. I went away very sad, though not surprised, that it was impossible for local church leaders to see a way to utilize my God-given time and talents as effectively as they utilize the treasure God has provided me.

And I was further saddened a few weeks later when our church had to hire a rather expensive outside consultant to conduct a drive for capital funds, much of which were spent simply to repair the roof and air-conditioner. While I continued to teach for other churches, civic clubs, and so on, it wasn't too much later that I began to look for another church, where I might be happier by utilizing my talents in the service of God. In that sense, I think I am a metaphor for millions of people in our churches today. And that is a major reason why many churches are filled with "God's frozen chosen" and why many denominations are in serious decline, particularly financially. (It might interest you that I've landed in an evangelical Lutheran church where I'm finding ample opportunities to work with leaders like Walt Kallistad in launching our own version of the Reformation!)

In moments of candor some of my clergy friends have told me they hesitate to utilize laity for church-related work within their chosen professions, as they're afraid the laity might profit financially in some way. It is surely one of the greatest ironies of modern religion that *professional* clergy *prevent* laypeople from utilizing their true God-given talents as they encourage us to more menial tasks such as planting flowers, moving tables, and so on. Michael Novak, a theologian who has won the Templeton Prize for Progress in Religion, described the clergy's attitude toward the gifts of businesspeople this way:

> Those whose religious and moral vocation in life is played out in one of the many fields of business get little enough help, then, from those they would normally turn to for instruction. Sometimes in sermons, pastoral letters, and other manifestoes of their churches, they get the impression that religious leaders don't object to wealth if it is inherited; in fact, they rather count on the largesse of established families of "old" money. But if you actually made the money yourself, in your own lifetime, maybe starting from nothing, you are given the subtle impression that

that, by contrast, is rather sweaty, vulgar, and morally suspect. The making of money is taken to be a sign of "materialism."[13]

Contrast that with Willow Creek Church, where I consult on a regular basis. Located outside Chicago, Willow Creek began as a youth ministry about fifteen years ago. Today it has sixteen thousand attendees and a debt-free facility valued in the tens of millions of dollars. Not coincidentally, it also has a lead pastor named Bill Hybels, who had the good sense fifteen years ago to ask people in his neighborhood why they didn't go to church. The results, which have been a case study at the Harvard Business School, showed that most people didn't go because churches are always asking for money. (Reasons number two and three were that churches are irrelevant and boring.) So Bill simply went back to the people and said he wouldn't ask for money until they had taken "Christianity 101" and grasped the paradox why giving is an integral part of the abundant life. When the *Chicago Daily Herald* profiled Willow Creek a decade ago, it observed, "The first thing most newcomers notice about Willow Creek is that no one asks them for money."[14]

In the tradition of the Reformation, Bill often says he isn't the minister but the person who trains the people sitting in the pews to be ministers. Consequently the church has established dozens of ministries, including one called the Good Sense Ministry. It consists of over 120 financial "counselors," some of whom are financial professionals and some of whom have simply lived within their means. These trained counselors daily help Willow Creek's members with credit card debt, budgeting, investments, and the spiritual dimensions of money. And each time I've been invited to speak there, they've asked me *not* to talk about giving money to the church but to help their members with their own finances.

There is undoubtedly a message for church leadership in that approach. In a particularly soul-searching article, the Rev. Loren Mead (who is a good friend but also ironically an Episcopal priest) of the Alban Institute, which specializes in church growth, has said,

Leading the fall stewardship campaign was often uncomfortable for me. In a sense I kept being aware that I was asking people to contribute to my salary, which usually was the biggest item in the budget. I was asking people to pledge to God, but I knew it was coming to me.... The fact is that money has more spiritual significance in the lives of people than almost anything else. If, indeed, clergy are caught up in debilitating binds about their relationship to money, they are handicapped in dealing with one of the most significant spiritual problems in their own life. And, if that is so, they are even more hindered in being of help to those in their congregations who likewise seek to understand what grace and forgiveness have to do with that portion of our life that we wall off as "money."[15]

Personally, I doubt most ministers can effectively deal with money any more than they can effectively lead the choir. It just doesn't seem to be their gift. But there's no reason why they couldn't imitate Bill Hybels and find someone in the church to lead a financial ministry. After all, financing God's work in the world is surely as important as singing his praises in church.

As instructive as all this has been, my primary way of looking at things was developed on Wall Street, where for twenty years I have helped people make investment decisions. As I spent the eighties in the great temples of Wall Street, I discovered our religion was very simple. We knew we served the god of money, and we were deeply devoted. If we failed to properly serve that god by making more money, that god simply closed those temples we called E. F. Hutton, Drexel Burnham Lambert, Thomson McKinnon, Integrated Resources, and so on, and moved the members to more effective temples of worship. As saddening as the eighties were in many ways, working in the churches of American Christianity during the nineties has been even more so—in fact, it has been quite probably depressing. While the church still helps my spirit soar in various areas of life, its approach to the "root of all evil" as worshiped in the other temples is to basically ignore it. And we aren't nearly as clear about what we believe, nor nearly as devout. We claim we know which God we serve, but our actions don't show the same devotion that I experienced on Wall Street.

As I considered leaving the Street for seminary in the mid-eighties, I realized I had never noticed *any difference whatsoever* in how believers and nonbelievers managed money. If any of my Christian clients had the final judgment in mind as we invested their one to five talents, I wasn't aware of it. If any of my fellow Christians on the Street had any interest in the topic, it wasn't evident. We pursued the same short-term rewards that everyone else did, a pretty good definition of secularists. And if any of us wanted to "serve God," we'd leave our "secular" occupations and head for seminary or a parachurch ministry, an approach too often encouraged by the clergy—even the Protestant clergy, which once staged the Reformation in resistance to clericalism on the part of the Catholic Church.

I've since served on the board of advisors of Bill Bennett and Jack Kemp's think tank called Empower America. Both have been active for many years in promoting more ethical ways of managing our nation's resources. Jack has long been a proponent of empowering our nation's poor and of "trade, not aid" with Third World countries. Bill has long encouraged our corporations to act more responsibly and has recently begun lobbying our large pension funds to divest themselves of companies that refuse. For example, he recently said this of Seagrams, a company that produces alcoholic beverages as well as hard-core music and videos: "Seagrams now joins other corporations in America in trying to make as much money as it can out of the wreckage of civilization. Their word is not worth anything."

And he has often connected the dots between *(a)* community breakdown and crime and *(b)* the marketing of alcoholic beverages. But how much success both Jack and Bill have experienced is unclear. Part of the reason is surely the lack of a similar devotion on the part of Christians in general. Peter Wehner, Bill's longtime assistant who now serves as Empower America's director of public policy, has recently observed, "It's unwise for Christians to keep averting our gaze from warnings that Christ placed in bright neon lights. . . . In pursuit of wealth and worldly possessions, Christians have become virtually indistinguishable from the rest of the world. We have bought into non-Christian precepts. Note the *irony:* Christians seeking and encouraging others to seek that which our Lord repeatedly warned against."[16]

That bit of reverse evangelization appeared in newspapers around our country. It is an example of a major problem that Christianity, and particularly conservative Christianity, has as we approach the year 2000. That problem is rightfully a major subtheme of this book. For if Jesus told us anything about money, it was that it will do us little good to gain the world but lose our souls (Mark 8:36).

Yet in recent decades we have funded and created tens of thousands of radio stations, television stations, and publications. We have funded tens of thousands of evangelists and stewardship leaders. The medium that we've built for spreading the gospel around the world is unparalleled in human history. But an increasing number of Americans and people around the world don't like the cultural message concerning money and power that they are hearing or seeing in the medium. We must wonder how much good news we are sharing when Christian psychologists, presumably looking out for our children, unwittingly spread economic paranoia that keeps us from investing for their futures; when Christian financial commentators spread fear and/or greed that keeps us from investing and giving; when Christian politicians organize us to seek the earthly power that Christ disdained; and when theologians help us escape our Christian responsibilities by teaching that the world is going to end soon, so there's no reason to bother with earthly matters.

In many ways, much of conservative Christianity has become what one of my friends calls the "Holy Huddle." To use another sports metaphor for our ministry leaders, or the men who often lead our team, like that little group on the football field each Sunday, we regularly gather round, pump each other up, and listen to a leader talk about what the Playbook says we should be doing. But to expand on the concept, the unfortunate part is that the fans—or the secularists and nominal Christians in the stands—aren't in on the huddle. They have little idea what our Playbook says. They're simply listening to the play-by-play on secular radio and television stations and reading the postgame analysis by secular newspapers and business publications. And none of this media is particularly interested that we're pumped when we're in the huddle. None really care what play we hope to execute when we come out of the huddle. They only care if we move the ball into the end zone by achieving both material and spiritual success. They, as well as Jesus, define that as "the abundant life," though Jesus might define *abundant* with greater spiritual balance.

We players, and especially team leaders, should be very aware that our perspectives of game conditions are confusingly different from the perspectives of those who sit in the stands and the press box. We often wonder what's wrong with these people. Yet they're doing a pretty admirable job of acting like nonbelievers. They often wonder what's wrong with our team, which isn't doing an equally admirable job of being "salt and light" in the world.

In many ways we are tremendously successful. But that very success makes for big problems. Almost by definition, we reach into our culture by evangelizing it. We have therefore helped millions to be "born again" as Christians. But these newly born-again Christians often remind me of myself twenty years ago when I was a newborn stockbroker. After a few months training with Merrill Lynch, I thought I had a thorough understanding of my new role in the world. I began a period of tremendous enthusiasm in the prospect of enriching the lives of everyone I came into contact with. Yet after ten years of my enthusiastically paving their roads to financial hell with my good intentions, I began to realize how very immature I had truly been and how very much I still needed to learn. It may well be the same with most immature Christians today.

We may not be quite as ready to shape the world's theology, manage our nation's economic policies, run our government, and dictate foreign policy as we have believed in recent years. That isn't to discourage enthusiasm on the part of the born-again. It is to encourage our leaders to channel our enthusiasms in directions more appropriate for immature believers, and probably for most believers in general. There are still plenty of poor to feed, naked to clothe, homeless to shelter, and imprisoned to visit. We have every skill needed to accomplish those wonderful things that preoccupied Jesus' time. Yet we have used valuable time on our airwaves proclaiming that the 1993 tax increase would devastate the economy; spending millions of dollars lobbying for a balanced budget amendment that we now realize was unneeded; trying to restrict trade with Eastern nations that once seemed threatening but now appear on the verge of bankruptcy; and so on. Why?

I've often thought "Mother Merrill," as the investment firm Merrill Lynch is known on the Street, could have encouraged a more realistic perspective concerning my new and rather limited skills. Then I might have channeled more of my client's money into mutual funds—where it would have been managed by true professionals equipped with the needed skills and experience—rather than into my futile efforts at trading stocks, buying limited partnerships, and so on. But I now understand that Mother Merrill had her own (financial) reasons for allowing me to be more impressed with my abilities than was appropriate. So despite the fact that many clients would have been more impressed had I been more humble, Mother Merrill gained some short-term benefit from my immature enthusiasm. In the same sense, religious leaders may have gained some (political) benefits from other immature enthusiasms in more recent years. Yet those benefits may also have been short-term in nature.

For example, many leaders of the Huddle are amazed when I explain that the *Wall Street Journal, Forbes,* and many thoughtful business leaders have maintained since the early nineties that the federal debt isn't that big a penalty, though it dominated the game plans of evangelical Christians during that period. Many very distinguished and conservative Christian investment professionals anticipated good playing conditions and rising markets during sunny economic weather when many evangelical leaders were gloomy over the debt. The result was that our leaders may have been achieving their own agendas, but many businesspeople in the stands and business writers in the press box often wondered why our offense had turned so defensive. We sometimes seemed so cautious about moving the ball toward the end zone that we didn't even seem happy to be playing the game. We seemed stalled. And the clock continued to move.

In a Golden Nugget

If we are to win this money game, we should take time out, sit down with the Coach, review the Playbook, study some films from recent games, and point out each other's errant throws, dropped passes, and missed blocks.

In a golden nugget, if we are to win this money game, we should take time out, sit down with the Coach, review the Playbook, study some films from recent games, and point out each other's errant throws, dropped passes, and missed blocks.

None of us needs to be proud over pointing them out or humbled by constructive criticism of our own fumbles. We've all dropped the ball plenty of times. We just need to learn from our mistakes, cover for each other's weaknesses, and together become a better team. Obviously, if some of us team leaders have long histories of bad calls on the economy, investments, or theology, the team might be more successful, and the fans more happy, if the Coach calls the plays from the sidelines.

The many ironies about our play in recent years have been well noted by those in the press box. And these ironies are keeping many people in the stands from becoming true fans or even joining our team. The approach of the year 2000 should encourage each of us to think about the fact that the end of the season is coming. That means gaining a new perspective or worldview. We'll soon have to sit down with the Coach and learn if we get to stay with the team ourselves, much less be proclaimed MVPs. We should quickly brush up on the play he called in Luke 18:9–14, about the Pharisee thanking God he was better than others simply because he fasted and tithed. Then we should review the one of Matthew 6:16–18, in which Jesus told us to keep *external* religiosities like fasting (bumper stickers, W.W.J.D. bracelets, T-shirts, etc.?) to ourselves so we can focus on the *internal* condition of our hearts, souls, and minds. And with our own nation in a moral crisis, we might particularly brush up on Matthew 23:15, where Jesus diagrammed the futility of evangelizing other nations when we should be saving ourselves. For that tunnel at the end of the field may prove narrow indeed once the game is over.

Three

Thinking About Money

More and more thought is being given to the future of the universe. We have a good idea how the universe began, but how will it end? What can we say about its ultimate fate? Will the universe finish with a bang or a whimper—indeed, will it ever end at all? And what of us? Can humanity or our descendants, be they robotic or flesh and blood, survive for all eternity? It is impossible not to be curious about such matters.

Paul Davies
The Last Three Minutes

The *Washington Times* has described Dr. Davies as "the best science writer on either side of the Atlantic." Professor of natural philosophy at the University of Adelaide, South Australia, Dr. Davies is the author of more than twenty books. While I have a university degree, have written a few books myself, and am considered fairly learned within my own profession, there were many parts of our conversation over dinner one evening that had me giving "more and more thought" to the end of our universe.

Have you ever heard that "ten thousand objects half a kilometer or more in diameter move on earth-intersecting orbits," that "many of these objects are capable of causing more damage than all the world's nuclear weapons put together," and that "it is only a matter of time before one strikes"? Dr. Davies can tell you even more fascinating and startling things of that nature. Had he and I not served on a board with Dr. Charles Townes, who won the

Nobel Prize for inventing the laser, I would say that Dr. Davies is probably the most brilliant scientist I have ever talked with.

Though you wouldn't expect a world-class scientist to be preoccupied with the end times, Dr. Davies' work in cosmology has received the serious attention of the religious community. He was awarded the 1995 Templeton Prize for Progress in Religion, the world's largest cash prize. It has also been awarded to more traditional religious leaders, such as Mother Teresa, Billy Graham, Chuck Colson, and Bill Bright, among others.

However, his statement that "science offers a surer path to God than religion" probably won't get him invited to many gatherings of religious fundamentalists. And you don't have to be a fundamentalist to wonder if what we *think* we know about our universe is a surer path to God than Holy Scripture and the Holy Spirit. Brilliant as they were, Galileo, Newton, and Bacon thought many things that modern scientists have found incomplete or have dispelled entirely. And I recently listened to an after-dinner talk in which Dr. Townes—who is so humble he even asks guys like me to call him Charlie—explained that many scientific phenomenon he observes each day seem beyond the laws of nature as we understand them. Like Jesus telling us to "look at the birds of the air," Dr. Townes encouraged each of us to learn from science but to resist placing too much faith in it.

As I finished reading Dr. Davies' brilliant observations about the nature of the cosmos and his speculations about its possible end, I found myself feeling a little empty. Though I'm sure the importance of his work is simply beyond my limited understanding, I still kept wondering, *So what? That's very interesting, and I'm glad that learned men like Dr. Davies understand such matters. But what do such speculations have to do with how I live my life?* In other words, I began to wonder about the rational perspective of modern science and the ultimate nature of things.

It was about that time that I read of Mother Teresa's death. She was a simple woman who would probably not have understood any more of Dr. Davies' theories than do I. And I doubt she would have spent much, if any, time trying. Yet she too was a recipient of the Templeton Prize. In fact, she was the first recipient twenty-five years ago. As the Prize was founded by John Templeton, I've tried to keep up with the various people who have received it, as well as why they've received it. It's been a fascinating study in how God works in mysterious and diverse ways.

As I write this chapter, the world is comparing the lives of Lady Diana and Mother Teresa. But being the contrarian that I am, I find myself reflecting on the lives of Mother Teresa and Dr. Davies. The judges for the Prize determined that both were tremendous stewards of their respective God-given talents. Yet I couldn't shake the notion that as important as it is to love God with heart, soul, and mind, the searching mind of Dr. Davies that is so knowledge-able of our universe doesn't seem as close to God as the loving heart of Mother Teresa that fed, clothed, and sheltered those who to her looked just like Jesus.

I feel that is an important way of looking at things from the Christian perspective. Notice that when Jesus commanded us to "love the Lord your God with all your heart and with all your soul and with all your mind" (Matt. 22:37) and to "love your neighbor as yourself" (Matt. 22:39), he put the heart, soul, and mind in the service of loving God and neighbor. At a later time the Scriptures say that if I "can fathom all mysteries and all knowledge . . . but have not love, I am nothing" (1 Cor. 13:2). And philosopher David Hume phrased the perspective as "reason must be the slave of the passions." In other words, all our thoughts must be directed toward the positive good that has captured our hearts—or in our Christian language, toward the establishment of the kingdom on earth.

Strange as it may seem, it is terribly important to put that into financial context if we want to make a little money without losing our souls. I remember that I once asked Sir John Templeton about the role of human reason in life. Though he was Phi Beta Kappa at Yale, a Rhodes Scholar, and arguably the most brilliant mutual fund manager of our age, he replied that his brain is a wonderful gift from God but is a very limited and temporary thing. That is why he has often told Wall Street that his financial success is due to his study of Scriptures, the power of prayer, and a generous helping of common sense, rather than a brilliant intellect. I would simply add that his loving ethic toward his neighbors around the world has also played a major role.

On Wall Street there's a new article of faith, probably a new religion, that says people should make financial decisions solely out of a "rational pursuit of self-interest." That is, most Americans are encouraged to simply use their minds to think about how their investments will bring the highest rewards to themselves. We are rarely encouraged to engage our hearts to evaluate how our investments are shaping the kingdom of God on earth. And our secular culture no longer encourages us to search our souls to determine if our investments might produce eternal rewards.

Despite being the lay leader of my local church, I bought into this new religion during the eighties. As I said in the introduction, I worked where I thought I could make the most money for myself. I associated with people because I thought they could help me make the most money for myself. And I invested where I thought I could make the most money for myself. So I now recognize people who have also been converted to the new faith, whether they know it or not. And I meet very, very few investors these days, Christian or otherwise, who do not practice the religion of the rational pursuit of self-interest—though we may have another mental compartment for charitable endeavors and our private business activities.

After twenty years of working with retired Christians in Florida, I'm still surprised at how we are often of two minds, seeing our private business activities from one perspective and seeing our activities in publicly traded businesses from a totally different perspective. Those of us who would never own a liquor store have few qualms about investing in the stocks of alcoholic-beverage companies. Others who would never sell lottery tickets in our gas stations have no qualms about investing in casino companies through our mutual funds. Some of us who would never sell *Playboy* in our grocery stores have no concerns that it is a prevalent stock in our pension funds. There are times, as with our 401(k) plans at work, when we seem to have little choice. Yet we don't seem to exercise that choice even when we can. And I have to believe that if the ninety percent of us who say we believe in God told Wall Street and our employers that we would like to exercise such choice, they might accommodate us.

On the other hand, we should never expect perfection in all our investments. Companies are simply groups of people and therefore prone to the imperfections of people. There's even an argument to be made that we should invest in most companies, even if we disagree with everything they do. For when we are owners, we have influence. We can go to the annual shareholders meetings, make speeches, vote on some matters, and so on. If we aren't owners, we have little or no influence in such matters. The dilemma is that the company whose *primary* business is one we question is not about to close its doors, no matter our influence. So my approach is to avoid those kinds of companies but invest in others that are generally beneficial, and influence them to brush up on the questionable areas. In other words, it is a financial expression of the old Serenity Prayer, which asks God to help us change the things we can, accept the things we can't, and have the wisdom to know the difference.

So with that perspective and my experiences on the farm of my youth, I have been particularly intrigued with the recent media coverage of the controversy over the cigarette industry. One of the things I noticed for several years was that the press was always quick to quote a Mormon mutual fund manager who is a strong proponent of owning shares of the industry but is quick to say he doesn't smoke. Ironically, in the early 1900s Mormons were primary instigators for the Pioneer mutual fund, and then several other funds, to shun the so-called sin stocks of alcohol, tobacco, and gambling companies.

I have not noticed a rush among Christians to bail out of funds that contain tobacco stocks. And the leading evangelical Christian mutual fund advisory letter in the country has run several features questioning the importance of ethics in the investment process. Both seem pretty good metaphors for the church's mixing the new cultural religion of the rational pursuit of self-interest with the tradition of using our hearts, souls, and minds for loving our neighbors as ourselves. It bears repeating what I said in the introduction: That mixing is a process theologians call "syncretism." And religious sociologist George Barna calls mixing the parts of Christianity we like with parts of other religions we like "the preferred religion of Americans."

Yet when the cigarette companies recently admitted that their products are unhealthy, probably deadly, for our neighbors, the *Wall Street Journal* ran two slightly different stories. One noted that the American Medical Association has been leading the charge to get investors to consider one of the dozens of mutual funds that do not finance the tobacco industry. They even provide "Good Housekeeping Seals of Approval" that tobacco-free funds can drop into their advertising. I thought how nice it would have been had the *Journal* told the business world that our churches, ministries, and financial newsletters had been leading the charge as well. Unfortunately, that same month I received a financial publication entitled *A Christian Perspective.* Published by a Christian stewardship foundation, it explained in detail why the foundation essentially ignored ethical funds when it made investment suggestions to its readers.

I reflected that Jesus once told a parable justifying a son who said he wouldn't do what the father wanted but did it anyway, yet condemning a son who said he would do what the father wanted but didn't (Matt. 21:28–31). And I wondered how Christ will judge the activities of the doctors of the American Medical Association and the stewards at the foundation and in our churches.

The other *Journal* article indicated that most mutual fund managers still do not see the issue as the AMA does. Beneath the headline "Few Mutual Funds Dump Tobacco Stocks," it described how most fund managers were just rationally calculating how much the tobacco industry might lose in the settlement and whether the industry would still make enough money to justify investing. The article added, "Fund industry giants Fidelity Investments and Vanguard Group are among the fund companies that have so far chosen not to include socially conscious funds in their extensive lineups. Fidelity managers are trying to earn the highest possible returns . . ."[1] A Vanguard spokesman essentially said that investors have differing ethics, so the company would not employ any ethics as it managed its customers' money. Higher returns rather than higher ethics, and/or dismissing ethics altogether, of course *are* the preferred ethics of a money culture. And from the perspective of the heart, none of the fund managers quoted expressed having any feelings about our neighbors who smoke—including many teenagers and increasingly the "least of these" around the world.

While the perspective taught by most fund companies is that we should simply *think* about making the most money possible, no-load funds such as Vanguard increasingly teach that we should also *think* about saving the most money possible. Either way, we are taught more and more that our investing should merely be about rationally pursuing the most money for ourselves.

While most fund companies like Fidelity teach that we can make more money if we don't engage our hearts in the investment process, Vanguard increasingly teaches that we can also make more money if we don't hire portfolio managers to use heart or mind in choosing what companies we want to finance. Vanguard index funds help us do that by simply buying shares of various-sized companies both here and abroad, simply because they're in an index rather than because they're producing beneficial goods and services for our neighbors. That *is* economical. And it has been rewarded in the long bull market of recent years. But so was thoughtlessly investing in highly leveraged real estate during the inflationary seventies—until the market turned against it. So we might wonder if investing in companies simply because they're in an index is another case of the most foolish approach looking smart in the short run.

Yet the index gospel is preached in some unlikely places. I recently visited two financial professionals who specialize in serving doctors and Christians. Health-related materials and religious books decorated their offices. They began to tell me how they were almost exclusively placing their clients' assets, which were in the hundreds of millions of dollars, into Vanguard index funds. When I asked why they chose that approach, they gave me a marketing piece that was highly critical of professionally managed mutual funds and explained how index funds have made more money at lower costs during the recent bull market. (Unfortunately, the marketing piece didn't say that when the professionals added their one percent annual fees to the costs of the funds, the net results for managing index funds were no better for the stock funds, than the professionally managed funds they had criticized, and adding that fee produced far worse returns for the bonds and money market instruments they watched over. As someone who can manage money for either fees or commission, I can assure you that's a good thing to remember. A significant percentage of index funds and no-load funds in general are marketed by fee-based advisors. Over the years the fees of the funds and the fee-based advisors can be *far more* expensive than simply buying a load fund, which involves commissions, through a broker who truly works to find superior funds and encourages you to stay with them for a while.

Yet what surprised me the most was that there was no ethic mentioned other than making the most money possible. This was probably because index investing guarantees we will own shares of companies engaged in activities we preach against in our churches and ministries, or at least used to, and doctors, educators, and other activists still preach against. For example, even a casual glance at its portfolio tells us the Vanguard S&P 500 Index Trust, which has quickly become the second-largest mutual fund in America, will make you a part owner of several alcohol, tobacco, and gambling companies; several companies engaged in the production of adult magazines and pornographic music; several companies whose environmental ethics are routinely questioned; several companies that manufacture the weapons many pacifists object to; Seagram's, which Bill Bennett says is helping destroy our civilization; and of course Disney, which the Baptists once boycotted for producing questionable entertainment and instituting questionable employment policies. So while we'll see later that a few good index funds do continue to engage the heart, Vanguard is convincing enormous numbers of normally thoughtful and caring people that it is smart if they no longer think or feel about the companies they own.

This too is a simple reflection of modernity. Much as some modern scientists teach a mechanistic view of the universe and encourage us to believe it operates like a clock with no need of God's grace, modern indexers teach that our investing should resemble an efficient computer with no need of our graceful touch as humans. I often hear the perspective that it doesn't matter, as we're small investors and our little bit of money doesn't make a difference in the scope of things. But reflect for a moment on the perspective of the legendary management consultant Dr. Peter Drucker, who has said, "If all the super-rich disappeared, the world economy would not even notice. The super-rich are irrelevant to the economy. The combined sources of money from the retail investors, pension funds and retirement plans of all individuals is the fastest-growing source of money. The *most important* source of capital is the average mutual fund transaction of $10,000."[2]

So I have to wonder if our children and our nation won't be better off if we all keep heart, soul, and mind in the investment process. The concept of stewardship would certainly benefit. And I wonder if we individual investors won't as well. Just a few years ago we used to hear that you couldn't lose with the famous "Nifty Fifty" stocks of the fifty largest corporations. Even investment professionals poured money into them without thinking about it. Yet those stocks decimated portfolios when the next recession arrived.

Today many index investors have essentially put the same faith in the Standard & Poor's 500 index of the five hundred largest corporations. The Vanguard S&P 500 Index Trust has now captured more assets in that single fund than John Templeton did in all his funds combined during forty years of ethical investing during the fat years and prudent investing during the lean years. Yet *Morningstar* recently said the index trust "will get creamed in a bear market,"[3] as many investors are no longer thinking about whether even excellent companies are worth forty to fifty times earnings, which is three or four times the historic norm.

It is ironic that some of us remember when John Bogle, the founder of Vanguard, built his business on the idea that it *is* a good idea to have professionals think about the companies investors should own. In fact, that is the foundational principle of the mutual fund industry. Yet the *Wall Street Journal* recently observed, "The market's relentless seven-year climb; the popularity of mutual funds; the shift by employers to self-directed retirement plans; and the avalanche of do-it-yourself investment publications all have combined to create a nation of financial know-it-alls."[4] An adjacent article even told of college students who managed imaginary portfolios. Their professor observed, "The students all come away thinking they're gifted."[5] It might be a good time to remember that old line "Pride goeth before a fall."

Another irony is that the brilliant and incredibly successful investor Warren Buffett recently told *Outstanding Investor Digest* about declining an investment in a chewing tobacco company that he knew would be very profitable. Demonstrating that his head is still connected to his heart, Mr. Buffett thoughtfully said every investor has to "draw the line" about ethics somewhere. His partner Charles Munger added, "I think each company and each individual has to draw their own ethical and moral lines. And personally, I *like* the messy complexity of having to do that. It makes life *interesting*."[6] And as new investors pile into stock index funds, *Forbes* and the *Wall Street Journal* have recently detailed that Mr. Buffett has decided it's a good time to buy some treasury bonds instead of stocks.

The irony continued when the *Journal* article compared the perspective of the Fidelity fund managers, who had been in the news for months because their funds were underperforming, with the perspective of another best-performing fund manager. He not only had used his brain to pick stocks for decades but had kept his heart and soul in the process as well. The article said,

> A couple of well-known fund groups, the Pioneer funds and Franklin Resources' Templeton funds, have been quietly shunning tobacco, alcohol and gambling securities for many years while not explicitly labeling themselves as socially active funds. The policy at Templeton "goes back to our founder, Sir John Templeton, who didn't invest in those stocks," says Don Reed, chairman of the portfolio management committee of the Templeton funds. "We don't think it necessarily has made any difference in our performance," he says, and some investors may not even know about this unwritten policy.[7]

Though he hadn't said a word, I thought that was another interesting piece of evangelization on Sir John's part to the people in the stands. It is one of many he has accomplished that reflect Saint Francis' perspective that we should preach the gospel continuously but use words only when necessary.

In my recent book *Ten Golden Rules for Financial Success,* about the spiritual and moral foundations underlying Sir John's way of looking at things, he said, "Ethics and spiritual principles should be the basis of all that we do in life, including the selection of investments." He elaborated that contrary to the common Wall Street perspective, he believes ethics probably enhance our returns, but had never wanted to say in public which industries he didn't feel were wise, as he had been taught not to judge his neighbors. He simply wanted to practice his own sense of ethics in his daily life as a money manager. I've always thought that is an admirable reversal of how I had looked at things when I was growing up on the farm and work-ing on Wall Street—as well as when I was working with some Chris-tian ministries.

As the tobacco wars have raged, several publications have noted that my Baptist family and friends are leading the ethical charge against Disney. As worthy as that issue may or may not be, an arti-cle headlined "A Real Boycott Takes Sacrifice" was syndicated in the *Los Angeles Times.* It contrasted this boycott with the Mont-gomery bus boycott that was sparked by the arrest of Rosa Parks and led by Martin Luther King, who was eventually assassinated for his vision of the kingdom of God. The article asked, "What will your boycotters be doing? Passing disdainfully by the Disney Store as they walk through the mall? Or making vacation plans that don't include Disney World? . . . A real boycott is about personal sacri-fice, not a change in entertainment plans."[8]

In a Golden Nugget

If anyone other than the referee is going to blow the whistle on unethical conduct, many people in the stands seem more impressed when we make the call on our own team.

So I was disappointed when the *Journal* article about the tobacco accord and fund managers noted that the Mormon manager was essen-tially rationalizing that if he didn't buy the tobacco companies, other investors would. And because I hear it all the time, I'm sure those managers would say, "Invest where you can make the most money, and give some of the profits to charity." But over the years I've noticed three very big problems with that perspective. First, assuming they make any more money—and that's a very big assumption—how many investors calculate it so they can give it away? Second, even if they did, how would we gain a more abundant life by investing in a tobacco company for the "extra" earnings and giving it to the American Cancer Society? And finally, if we look at it in the eternal context, will Jesus say it was fine for us to sin because someone was going to and it might as well have been us?

It will strike most fund managers as an odd way of looking at things, but in what must have been the result of much soul-searching, Sir John has said, "I've helped thousands of people with their investments, but in the over-all scheme of things, is it really important that a group of people is somewhat more prosperous as a result?"

My opinion is that Sir John is too humble. As the dean of global investing, he essentially pioneered the concept that wealthy North Americans might prosper by financing the industries that will meet the material needs of the less fortunate around the world. Yes, I think that is important. But I've greatly respected the fact that through the years, numerous people in the stands have witnessed that same soul-searching perspective of what Sir John believes is of even greater importance. For example, against background music of "Amazing Grace," he once told viewers of *Lifestyles of the Rich and Famous* that he didn't collect yachts or airplanes, only antique Bibles. And he has repeatedly told brokers that the best investment he has ever made has been his tithe. That way of looking at things is pretty rare in today's money culture. It will look better when we meet with the Coach at the end of the season.

———————————

To help us see things from the perspective of eternity, Barbara Walters has often asked famous people how they want to be remembered after they are gone. *U.S. News & World Report* remembered Mother Teresa this way:

Mother Teresa refused to solicit funds. Asking where the money came from invariably drew the same laconic reply:

"The Lord provides." That he does—through a support network that ranges from schoolchildren saving their coins to the wealthy salving their consciences. In 1992, for example, she flew to New York to be presented with a $100,000 award by the Knights of Columbus. At a white-tie banquet attended by 1,000 members of America's Catholic elite, Mother Teresa was accorded the kind of roaring adulation normally reserved for rock stars or the pope. Before the feast began, the diminutive nun chastened the throng by describing how it took her three hours to pick maggots from the body of an emaciated Calcutta derelict. Then, as was her custom, she left before eating because she felt it inappropriate to dine ostentatiously. An additional $100,000—equal to the cost of the banquet—was later presented to her. The Lord provides.[9]

The Associated Press remembered her this way:

In a week when the leader of one of the United States' largest Baptist churches publicly sought forgiveness for moral lapses, [Note: These have been on the front pages of my local papers for weeks and were mostly about alleged financial improprieties] and at a time when nearly all religious leaders seem to be drawn into political minefields, her work picking up the dying off the streets of Calcutta or rescuing mentally ill children in Beirut captured the world's imagination of one person who embodied the religious ideal of simple, selfless service to the poor.[10]

While Mother Teresa wouldn't want me to feel this way, I felt crushed by the irony that I spend much of my life both attending stewardship banquets and trying to figure out how to encourage people to give to ministry. Yet Mother Teresa never had to ask for money. She rarely spoke from pulpits, talked on the radio, or wrote for religious publications as I do. But she evangelized the world in a way I can't begin to imagine, by seeking first the kingdom and trusting God to add to her the resources she needed.

Now, looking forward, we shouldn't ignore the example of Dr. Davies, who reminds us that we are also called to the "mind of Christ" (1 Cor. 2:16). For while allowing the heart to get disconnected from the mind can create warm and fuzzy feelings, it can also create enormous problems. And that's a rather common occurrence when religious leaders, and therefore many Christians in general, begin talking about the emotionally charged subject of money and especially how it might relate to the end of things as we know them.

Four

Feeling the Pains and Joys of Money

> *How close are we to Armageddon? As we approach the year 2000, this question looms larger in the minds of many people. This book is an attempt to provide an answer. At no time since Jesus ascended to heaven have so many remarkable events and trends come together—events and trends predicted in the Bible to be features of the end-times. How close are we? Closer than you may think!*
>
> ED DOBSON
> *THE END*

Christianity Today recently described the Rev. Dobson as a former lieutenant in Jerry Falwell's Moral Majority, former editor-in-chief of the *Fundamentalist Journal,* and current senior pastor of the six-thousand-member Calvary Church in Grand Rapids, Michigan.[1] Unlike most conservative church leaders, he is well known and respected in his city's gay and lesbian community and challenges his congregation to minister to the social needs of that community. In other words, he has that rare quality of conservative theology with a heart for the poor and oppressed.

My fear, however—and it applies to most all who see the end around the corner—is that he pays too much attention to his feelings when it comes to eschatology. And if there's one thing that has kept millions of conservative Christians from making a little money without losing their souls during the nineties, it has been some leaders' ability to look at facts and hold to their feelings that the world is ending, regardless of what the facts say.

In 1994 I was invited to debate a Christian businessman who had just participated in one of the most pessimistic economic videos I have ever seen. It was called *The Crash: The Coming Financial Collapse of America* and featured Christian financial advisor Larry Burkett as well as some conservative politicians. I was startled when the businessman began our debate by saying he expected to lose the debate, as I had on my side all the facts, which would "confuse" the listener, and all he had was "truth on his side." (The video too claimed "the truth" about America's "economic crisis."[2]) As the debate began, the host wondered how we could possibly look at the same economic statistics and come to such diametrically opposed conclusions. The listeners were probably equally confused.

But it quickly became evident that the businessman hadn't been looking at any facts that might transform his mind, in Paul's words, other than the size of the federal debt, which affirmed his *feeling* that the world was about to end. As we proceeded, he admitted that he had never heard the size of America's assets. So he was essentially paranoid about his mortgage bankrupting him without ever determining the value of his home. He had never heard that our federal-debt-to-national-income ratio was half of what it was at the end of World War II and one-fourth of what Great Britain's was. He refused to believe that at that time about ninety percent of America's federal debt was owed to Americans, who received the interest payments. (About eighty percent of it is today.)

In essence, our government can be in debt without our nation being in debt, as the money has been borrowed from our fellow Americans. If we insist on looking at it from our own small perspectives, it is as though we have borrowed our mortgage from our own IRAs and are therefore paying ourselves the interest and principle. That may not be an ideal use of our IRAs, as they could be more productively invested. But it's also far better than borrowing our mortgage from others.

Yet none of these facts seemed to phase him. After hearing each one, he insisted we were "doomed" and suggested our audience shouldn't listen to such facts. I left the debate wondering why he had made a video that had really scared a lot of people, if he didn't care about the facts of the matter. As the markets soared in coming years, I reflected that letting a few facts into our minds might not be such a bad thing if we hope to make a little money without losing our souls, even if those facts disagree with "the truth" we vaguely feel we know in our hearts.

So I was interested that chapter 1 of the Rev. Dobson's book is entitled "The End of the World as We Know It." It is a good indication that we have learned little and that these vague feelings, rather than facts, continue to dominate our worldview as we approach the year 2000. Despite fundamentalists' deep suspicions of modern science, the chapter's primary argument concerns the famous doomsday clock maintained by the *Bulletin of the Atomic Scientists*. The Rev. Dobson notes that when the clock was introduced in 1947, it showed *seven* minutes to midnight, or doomsday. In 1953 the scientists set the clock at *two* minutes to midnight. Dr. Dobson then notes that after several nuclear arms treaties in recent decades, the last setting was made in 1995 at *fourteen* minutes to midnight. Yet he concludes, "The world remains moments from nuclear disaster and the situation is getting worse—not better."

I hope this criticism is offered in a constructive sense, but that way of looking at things will do little to persuade today's more rationally scientific baby boomers to join our team. Yet despite possibly keeping people in the stands rather than in the game, it is the kind of perspective that seems to creep into end-times theology, and into conservative theology in general, far too often. We should be more careful. As we approach the year 2000, baby boomers are searching for greater meaning in life and need to hear that life is more abundant when lived with an eye to eternity. But we'd better have our facts straight and our conclusions coherent. Boomers are smart—and very skeptical of institutions like the church.

Yet if Dr. Dobson has a little weakness in scientific observation, he has great strength in observing how conservative Christians relate to money and the end times. He writes,

> I am concerned that when it comes to money and material things, we live as if there is no eternity and no hope of the coming of Jesus. We are self-indulgent and hoard our resources for our own benefit rather than investing them for kingdom purposes. We believe in the Second Coming. We believe that our stewardship will be judged. But we actually live as if God did not exist and Jesus was in fact not coming. I would say that makes us *eschatological atheists!*[3]

Other conservative Christian leaders see the same thing when they look around. (That should give us pause if it's true that we see things not as they are but as we are.) When *Christianity Today* recently reviewed three end-times books, it concluded,

> On the evidence assembled here, key evangelical leaders have lost all confidence in the institutional church, seeing God at work exclusively with individuals and focused para-church ministries. This disdain for the church is accompanied by a *preoccupation with evangelism as the only legitimate work of the Christians.*[4]

Ironically, the Protestant Reformation was largely about "the priesthood of all believers" reclaiming a sense of ministry from professional clergy who had taken it hostage. It was a central contention of Martin Luther and other reformers that there is nothing more holy about a minister preaching about the Good News than men and women living it by using their resources of time, talent, and treasure in the tending of fields and homes for the glory of God and love of families and neighbors. Yet the *Wall Street Journal* recently made this observation of today's Pentecostals working in Latin America:

> The persistent message from the pulpit stresses the importance of being "called" by God to the "full-time ministry."

The only people who are really doing "God's work" are evangelists, teachers and the like. Such nonministers as carpenters,
housewives, doctors and politicians, when they become Pentecostals, risk being second-class citizens in the "Kingdom of
God." If there is no future (the world's end is imminent), why
bother with these "temporal" pursuits?[5]

This emotional way of looking at things has enormous implications not only for how we manage our time and talents but for how
we manage our money. *Christianity Today* and the *Journal* indicate
"evangelism is the only legitimate work of the Christians" as the
world winds down. So we shouldn't be too surprised when evangelical leaders imply that the only legitimate use of money is for their
evangelistic endeavors in the very near future. And we're going to see
repeatedly that this way of looking at things is shared quite often in
American Christianity, particularly evangelical Christianity.

But before we look at that, we should note the irony that after
telling the parable of the talents, which encouraged the general pro-
ductivity of the resources entrusted to our care, Jesus spent the rest
of Matthew 25 providing some details about his perspective of
what it means to be productive. This passage is often referred to as
the final judgment or the division of the sheep and goats. It will
come as a great surprise to many evangelical and Pentecostal Christians that *Jesus doesn't even mention* that preaching the gospel to the
ends of the earth is a criteria that will determine the fate of our
souls. While I may quibble at the Rev. Dobson's questionable
assessment of scientific facts to predict the return of our Lord, I
applaud him for breaking away from the other "end-timers" by
focusing on what really matters:

People will be measured by what they did for the hungry, the
thirsty, the homeless (the "stranger"), the naked, the sick and
the prisoners. . . . Those who take care of these people will be
invited into the kingdom. Those who ignored them will be

"cursed" and thrown into "the eternal fire prepared for the devil and his angels." ...

When we face Jesus in judgment, we will be reckoned by how we treated the needy people God brought our way. Jesus is not teaching a way of salvation by social responsibility. We are saved exclusively by faith. Rather, he is teaching that a *saving* faith [Dobson's emphasis] is one that is translated into action. Too many of us evangelical Christians have *completely lost* [emphasis mine] the social implications of the gospel.[6]

In a golden nugget, many evangelicals preoccupied with preaching to the world, and many fundamentalists preoccupied with the Second Coming, are precisely the most likely to be "completely lost" about Christ's message concerning the final judgment.

Most evangelical stewardship is really fund-raising and is therefore disconnected from the Rev. Dobson's view of how we will ultimately be

In a Golden Nugget

Many evangelicals preoccupied with preaching to the world, and many fundamentalists preoccupied with the Second Coming, are precisely the most likely to be "completely lost" about Christ's message concerning the final judgment.

judged. For example, for several years I have addressed a large evangelical stewardship group. Though they use the word *stewardship* in their name, they virtually never talk about anything but fund-raising. As last year's evangelical stewardship meeting neared, I knew everyone else would focus on fund-raising. So I prepared to talk about the economy, trends in wealth, ethical and spiritual principles, and most anything but pledge cards and charitable trusts. Yet I began by quoting a major study that found people cite economic pessimism over the future as the single largest deterrent to their charitable giving. I then showed chart after chart, from very conservative sources, that showed wealth was growing faster and faster despite the perception, often shaped on conservative Christian radio, that we're going broke. And I explained how ethics and spiritual principles like hope and gratitude had turned Sir John Templeton into a major funder of religious causes. Several weeks later I received the evaluation cards that participants were asked to fill out. My overall rating was a solid A–. Yet the area that about half of them found weakest was the "usefulness of the information in your work." Of all people, we just don't seem to get it.

While there are certainly admirable exceptions, it is quite possible that if you read and listen to many evangelical stewardship leaders, you may never hear them discuss even one practical financial concept. You may also never hear them discuss one way for you to be of personal service to the poor. And no institution on earth, whether governmental or ministerial, should keep you from the blessing of *personally* loving those our Master most closely identified with. They can teach us much about true faith in God. Their spirit of overcoming true challenges can free those of us choked by modern trivialities. And they can remind us how very materially blessed we are in America. Yet as much as it embarrasses me, I've been openly criticized as being a liberal after discussing on Christian radio *nongovernmental* ways of helping the poor to help themselves.

In a Golden Nugget

While we evangelicals are wonderfully efficient (at least compared with the rest of Christianity) at funding the Great Commission, too often we are content to simply encourage giving.

In a golden nugget, while we evangelicals are wonderfully efficient (at least compared with the rest of Christianity) at funding the Great Commission, too often we are content to simply encourage giving to ministries while ignoring all the rest.

As terribly important as evangelism is, what we say in the Huddle or to the people in the stands has never been the criteria by which Jesus will measure our play on the field. He is more interested in how we move the ball toward the end zone. If that sounds like some personal frustration on my part, it is. I normally have no problem challenging the way Wall Street teaches us to look at things. But it becomes virtually impossible to help people see things in an eternal context when Christian leaders baptize cultural ideas such the notion that fear and greed should motivate where we invest or that God is only interested in ten percent of our income and could care less about how the principle is employed. *The Christian way of seeing things has always been that God owns one hundred percent of everything, not two percent, or even ten percent, of the income that it produces.* And God wants us motivated by a sense of ethics at a minimum and a sense of sacrificial love as an ideal. We must never create man-made theological walls—which are the very thickest walls I deal with daily—around ninety-eight percent of our resources by constantly implying that God is interested in anything less than one hundred percent of them.

Again, the irony is that reality sends a far clearer message to those in the stands. A reporter from a secular newspaper recently asked an evangelical stewardship leader if he could explain the difference between philanthropy and Christian stewardship. The leader replied, "Christian stewardship is all about God. God provides resources to people, these people see themselves as managers (not owners) of God's resources, they choose to *give a portion* back to God, they *give to ministries* that advance the work of God, and they recognize that God will ultimately acknowledge the giving they did in this life and in the life to come."[7]

I happen to greatly respect this particular leader. We've had conversations about the need for evangelicals to be more holistic in their thinking. But I can understand why the reporter was having trouble seeing any difference in the way we Christians manage money. That statement contains some *beliefs* about eternity that differ from the beliefs of our secular culture. Yet the only difference in *action* in this life seems to be that secular philanthropists give a little to museums and the Red Cross, while Christian stewards give a little to churches and World Vision. I believe the secularists of our world will better understand the Christian perspective if we'll help them see things this way, as I developed it after reflecting on the differences in stewardship and philanthropy:

> Christian stewardship is all about God's love for me and there-fore my love for my neighbor. God entrusts me with the resources of time, talent, and treasure, as well as the freedom to manage all of them productively, a portion of them produc-tively, or to totally waste them. Financially, philanthropists can get by with giving a *portion of their incomes* to worthy causes. Stewards are required to *manage all God's resources—both prin-ciple and income*—for our neighbors as well as ourselves in the co-creation of the kingdom. A part of that management con-cerns giving a portion of my income to ministries, but Jesus said it especially concerns my *giving to the poor*. Frankly, it's a whole lot easier to simply be a philanthropist, or even a Chris-tian philanthropist who gives a portion of his income to wor-thy Christian causes. But Jesus never promised that true stewardship would be easy. He only promised that it would be worth it for all eternity when we're judged faithful and grace-ful stewards rather than partial donors.

Now, don't get me wrong. I strongly believe that tithing at least ten percent of our income is the single most important aspect of stewardship. And it is crucial that some of it be used for the health of our churches, colleges, and ministries, as they are vital for the moral and spiritual health of our nation and world. But we must never forget that Jesus used frightening language as he told the Pharisees they could tithe the "mint, dill and cumin" from the gar-den and still miss the important teachings of the faith (Matt. 23:23). We should always remember that although *Forbes* recently said that "worthiness of goal" is by far the single largest motivation for Americans' giving, Jesus wasn't particularly concerned with the worthiness of the masses but gracefully gave his time, talents, and love. And Jesus' admiration of the widow and her mite, rather than the wealthier businesspeople and their larger donations, should keep us "major donors" most humble. It should not be so difficult to find that compassionate, graceful, and humble perspective in evangelical stewardship circles.

In a golden nugget, some of us caught up in a single-minded financing of the Great Commission to spread the gospel of Christ to the ends of the earth don't always see that the gospel of Christ is about financing the needs of those who are all around us!

Too often we settle for the means (developing the medium for preaching the gospel) rather than the end (actually living the gospel). And that's why so many people in the stands, and increasingly our own team members, are disappointed that we often simply huddle and call plays about what needs to happen. We even tell the guys in the stands what we hope to do. But too often we no longer move the ball toward the end zone of the abundant life.

In a Golden Nugget

Some of us caught up in a single-minded financing of the Great Commission to spread the gospel of Christ to the ends of the earth don't always see that the gospel of Christ is about financing the needs of those who are all around us!

That difficult reality often puts me in tension with even the most respected leaders. Even they can become so single-minded in their life's work that they obscure the financial teachings of Jesus and thus pave the road to hell with good intentions. Consider this financial perspective from Bill Bright, one of the best-known and best-intentioned evangelical leaders. In an article under the headline "A Serious Countdown," he recently asked his supporters to

reflect that "we have only 1,340 days before the year 2000," a year
in which "we expect by faith to complete the Great Commission."
He then said, "If you really take seriously the Great Commission,
if you agree with me that the greatest thing that ever happened to
you is knowing Christ as your Lord and Savior, and if the greatest
thing you could do to help another person is to help them know
Christ, then sell your stocks and bonds and real estate and whatever
else God has put in your possession, and after making proper financial arrangements for your family, invest the rest of your assets in
helping to fulfill the Great Commission."[8]

That's a wonderful sentiment from the heart. But when one
financially astute theologian reviewed this manuscript, he thought
it financially challenged and wrote in the margin, "No, it's not. It's
stupid!" In other words, and with all respect to Dr. Bright, even a
little logic tells us that "making proper financial arrangements for
your family" probably means rebuying some of the stocks, bonds,
and real estate that you just sold. Selling them all could also dis-
rupt the economy and bankrupt a lot of investors, financial planners, brokers, and bankers who are loyal supporters of many
ministries, some of which have a game plan for the next century
just in case the world doesn't end in the year 2000, which Dr.
Bright did acknowledge might occur, though this concession came
much later in his article. (And the possibility that the end is perhaps
not quite so near is perhaps more evident by the fact that Campus
Crusade is building a new world headquarters, which will presumably be of as much use in the next millennium as our own real
estate like factories, farms, and homes might be!)

While such a self-centered if well-intentioned message might
help evangelical leaders meet budgets in the short run, it is unlikely
to appeal to the rest of us in the long run. So since we're tempted to
share such emotional perspectives as we approach the year 2000, we
might remember two other views: First, many theologians believe
that the earliest church suffered a depression in Jerusalem because
they thought the world was about to end and there was no need to

think about the future. Some even believe Saint Paul took time from his evangelism to take up the Great Collection because he had something to do with creating that depression. And second, Christ never said, "Sell what you have and give it to an evangel" any more than he said, "Sell what you have and give it to the church."

In what may be as relevant today as it was centuries ago, the *Didache: The Doctrine of the Twelve Apostles,* which was so influential in second-century Christianity, offered this way of looking at things: "And every prophet that teaches the truth, if he does not what he teaches is a false prophet.... Whosoever shall say in the spirit: Give me money, or any other thing, ye shall not listen to him: but, if he bid you give for others that are in need, let no man judge him."[9]

Our ministries obviously have many legitimate needs. Many are on behalf of others we serve. But that passage might be most useful in helping us steer clear of those whose only financial perspective is to see the needs of their own ministries. For they obviously do not see things as God has over the centuries.

One reason for such shortsightedness and self-centeredness may be that we evangelicals aren't sure adequate resources are available for funding both the Great Commission and our responsibilities to the poor into the future. Ironically, that may be due to the doom-and-gloom economic perspective that has dominated the evangelical media for much of this decade and for many decades in the past. Studies consistently say economic pessimism is one of the greatest deterrents to charitable giving in our country. Yet anyone who listens to Christian radio is acutely aware that America has a $5 trillion federal debt. And I have never met *any* listener who knows we have from $55 trillion to $110 trillion in assets, depending on whether we accept our government's estimate or the World Bank's estimate. (Private estimates usually fall somewhere between the two.)

Most listeners have heard that our government estimates that our federal debt may reach over $200 trillion by the middle of the next century. But few have heard that the government also estimates that our annual income may reach $80 trillion. That means our debt-to-income ratio may rise from its current 50 percent to about 250 percent as boomers age and count on health care, retirement benefits, and so on. That is surely troubling. Yet it is still about where Great Britain's was at the end of World War II, so prudence rather than panic is in order. And we should note that for several years both governmental and private economists have overestimated our deficits and underestimated our growth. How much better they can be at predicting both well into the next century is questionable. A little humility about our ability to see into the future might focus our attention more on the problems at hand, which are moral and spiritual. Paradoxically, that might brighten the econonic future.

In a Golden Nugget

It is one of the great ironies of American Christianity that studies consistently say economic pessimism is a major deterrent to charitable giving and investing for the future, yet we have filled our media with talk about economic earthquakes, financial holocausts, and Armageddon rather than the counting of our blessings.

Due to such confusion in our materialistic culture, I know many Americans don't feel very blessed today. But my work over the past twenty years indicates there is very little connection between how people feel and their actual circumstances. And one very fundamental aspect of modern capitalism is to have advertising stimulate the perceived needs of people so they are never satisfied with what they have. That's another good reason why capitalism needs a spiritual dimension. But that doesn't keep publications like the *Economist* from detailing the fact that on average we enjoy about $27,000 of purchasing power versus around $4,500 at the turn of the century. And that is after adjusting for inflation. That undoubtedly puts us in the top one percent of all consumers in human history.

In a golden nugget, it is one of the great ironies of American Christianity that studies consistently say economic pessimism is a major deterrent to charitable giving and investing for the future, yet we have filled our media with talk about economic earthquakes, financial holocausts, and Armageddon rather than the counting of our blessings.

And it's doubtful that the more recent greedy perspectives will do any more to open our hands for ministries, the poor, and prudent investments, though they might keep donations pouring in to the few ministries and politicians who preach such perspectives.

In summary, many of us seem rather like the priest who hurried by and left the injured fellow for the Good Samaritan to take care of. We get so passionate about running around preaching our *feelings* that the world is ending that we can't slow down long enough to *think* that America's balance sheet has a very rich positive side. The facts say that we are rich enough to fulfill the Great Commission to evangelize the world *and* the Great Commandment to love our neighbors as ourselves. Our hearts just need to be free of those feelings of economic fear and greed. And our lives need to be open to the spirit of plenty. That is the spirit that fed the multitudes both the material loaves and fishes and the spiritual Beatitudes on the mount two millennia ago. It would be wonderful if we could catch that spirit as we approach another millennia.

Five

The Spirit of Money

The church was not formed to manage the property of its members, or to command their charitable efforts; nor can it show any commission to that effect. You are a steward not for the church, but for God. The property which you have, or may have in possession, belongs to you; as an individual and not as a member of the church; and you as an individual, must account for it to the supreme proprietor.

LEONARD BACON
THE CHRISTIAN DOCTRINE OF STEWARDSHIP
THE YEAR 1832

History is replete with examples of the church losing its spiritual balance from time to time. Currently we're living in one of the most materialistic ages in history, and it seems the church is as caught up in this spirit as the rest of us. During most of the nineties, our evangelical ministries have often focused on the material problems of America. Yet, ironically, we also appear to be so concerned with the legitimate spiritual needs of our neighbors around the world that we've lost sight of their material needs.

How did our perspective get so out of balance? I believe it began in the early 1900s, when mainline and Catholic Christianity began to focus primarily on the social gospel. This encouraged them to build hospitals, soup kitchens, and so on. Early evangelicals essentially disagreed with their priorities, as they rightfully knew that action without faith is dead. In other words, evangelicals knew that mainline charities could build soup kitchens to eternity but many people could find the abundant life if their hearts were transformed and empowered by a true and lively faith. Unfortunately, over the decades since, many mainline and Catholic Christians have lost much of their ability to evangelize. Those, like Mother Teresa, who have continued their social activities have prospered. Those who have lost the ability to evangelize and lost their social activities to government are increasingly seen as irrelevant and are watching their team shrink. Meanwhile evangelicals are growing in numbers but often appear ineffective in our political economy.

If religion were industry, this arrangement would be known as the "division of labor." That's an economic principle that says we all have particular talents and should stick with them. It is a fundamental tenet of capitalism and is therefore a strong cultural influence. And it is a marvelously efficient principle in industry. But I believe it is an ineffective principle in ministry. For workers must coordinate their skills on our assembly lines and in our economy. But you'll rarely find a mainline Christian doing social work who is cooperating with an evangelical who is preaching the gospel. This is despite the Scriptures asking us to be of one mind and one spirit (Phil. 2:1–2).

Consider one very real case of how our schizophrenic spirit limits our ability to help the world make a little money without losing its soul. I once went to Uganda at the invitation of the Church of England and the Church of Uganda. Uganda was preparing for a constitutional convention after Idi Amin had destroyed it. One of the churches' greatest concerns was that Islam was making deep inroads into Africa because that religion proclaimed access to both bread and salvation. (Islam is very popular with many Third World political leaders due to its habit of building mosques next to Islamic banks which still do not, at least technically speaking, believe in charging on loans the interest that burdens many Third World nations.)

There were several mainline social workers there caring for orphans and so on. But they weren't capable of communicating how true Christianity provides at least as many moral foundations on which to build a successful political economy as Islam does. And there were plenty of evangelicals preaching the gospel, but they seemed to know little about helping the Ugandans create wealth.

This schizophrenic spirit limits Christianity's appeal at home as well. This is the "Decade of Evangelism" in the Episcopal Church. When it was first announced in the early nineties, I irreverently quipped to a friend that this meant we would spend the decade trying to figure out what the word *evangelism* means. Since I haven't heard anything about the subject since about 1992, I was probably optimistic in hoping for even that!

You can observe another dimension of the problem by exploring several end-times books, written by evangelicals, that are also highly political in nature, short on financial wisdom, and therefore unlikely to draw most spiritual seekers out of the stands and onto our team. When *Christianity Today* recently spoke with Pat Robertson concerning his new book entitled *The End of the Age,* he shared this perspective of the church he sees each day (though he might see a quite different church among the Amish, Mennonites, Catholic sisters who have taken vows of poverty, and other religious folk I often have the pleasure of serving): "I think the church is very, very carnal and very, very self-centered. It's almost impossible to get money for missions in America. You can get money for a new basketball court in a church or pave the parking lot or put in a new organ, but it's almost impossible to get people to give to relief efforts overseas."[1]

Yet when *Christianity Today* asked him what needed to be done in the near future, his game plan was: "I want Christians to be energized to do the work of the Great Commission, that they should use their time, their energy and their money to accomplish this task. There's an imperative to evangelize the world now."[2] I serve a ministry that has utilized a generous gift from Pat to empower many poor people around the world, so I know Pat has a heart for the "least of these." But it still seems that evangelism is our predominant focus when we look overseas.

Too often we send our missionaries out with the zeal of cavalry troops rushing to save the world. Yet tens of millions of those 1.3 billion people who live on about one dollar per day have counted on their faith to keep them alive during persecutions few American Christians can begin to imagine. In Uganda alone, we were shown rooms where perhaps one million people were shot or castrated by Idi Amin for little reason other than being Christian. Yet one young political leader, who was also a leader in their Christian church, told me that if he becomes president one day, his first act will expel one of our best-known evangelical ministries because of the perceived arrogance of the people it has sent to his country. He told me a sad story of the ministry's last missionary buying one of the grander homes in the country and hiring Ugandans at very low wages to do his housekeeping and so on. In short, our affluent, western economic perspective had again done little to gain a few souls in a nation very sensitive to anything smacking of colonialism.

We should always remember that there are 260 million Americans who on average enjoy purchasing power of over *fifty times* what those 1.3 billion people live on. Even those Americans who make minimum wage and work forty hours per week enjoy over *twenty times* as much purchasing power as do the "least of these," many of whom work far longer hours. Yet giving to "benevolences" outside our local churches amounts to approximately one-half of one percent of our incomes and was about fifty percent higher when I was in high school. And experts say relatively little of even that reaches the "least of these" around the world, even though many of the "least of these" sit in Christian churches each week.

Studies tell us that most Americans have developed the perspective that our government is caring for those 1.3 billion people. Reality is that U.S. foreign aid amounts to under one-tenth of one percent of our national income. That is the lowest of all major nations on earth and has been the lowest for many years now. And a very large part of that goes to Israel and Egypt for largely political purposes. I'm not advocating more foreign aid on the part of our government. But I am advocating that every American Christian shed the illusions that obscure the issue, and explore the options that will meet the needs of the "least of these"—and if we really believe the end is near, we ought to proceed with great haste.

We should also be aware that politics has played a major role in shaping our materialistic spirit. I recently attended a board meeting of a ministry I serve. It was held at Pat Robertson's Founder's Inn. A young bellman picked me up at the airport. We were the only people in the van back to the Inn, so we had a nice conversation. He was a bright young man and was very interested in my profession, as his goal in life is to one day give one billion dollars to Christian ministry. (Though raising one billion dollars for Christian ministries is also the often cited goal of a well-known evangelical stewardship leader, there is little evidence that Jesus ever wanted such goals to define our religious lives. If anything, Jesus seemed deeply concerned about those who did. And historical figures like Tetzel have repeatedly justified his concerns.)

When he asked about my views on the stock market, I told him I was concerned at its lofty levels. He then asked what he might do with a little IRA money. I suggested he consider putting some of it into mutual funds that might take advantage of cheaper markets around the world, and by extension enrich those less fortunate than ourselves. He then asked, "Isn't that un-American?"

I was reminded that only a couple of years ago Pat Buchanan wrote a major editorial in the *Wall Street Journal*. Beneath the headline "An American Economy for Americans," Mr. Buchanan shared his perspective that America was going broke, and described his plan for us to "work, save and invest here in the land of the free." He then asked, "Who, after all, is the American economy for, if not for Americans?"[3]

Looking at things from an even narrower perspective, I assume I could also ask, "Who, after all, is Gary's work for, if not for me?" But I simply said to my new friend, "Yes, I guess that if you look at things from a political perspective, you might see things that way.

But if you look at things from God's perspective, you would be concerned for your own nation, but you might also be equally concerned for our neighbors around the world." I then shared biblical stories—such as the ones about Joseph in Egypt, the building of the temple, the Good Samaritan, and Saint Paul's Great Collection—in which Jews and Christians crossed political barriers to do business and help one another. Had I had a little more time, I would have also reminded him that our country quite probably wouldn't have won the Revolutionary War without the help of the French Marquis de Lafayette and the Prussian Baron von Steuben, and that European money financed our railroads and canals during the nineteenth century when America was considered a developing nation.

But I mostly wondered why, if we Protestants truly believe in the ministry of all believers, we feel compelled to send our ordained missionaries and gospel abroad but keep our businesspeople and dollars at home.

My new friend replied that he had never looked at things that way. Neither do many people I meet each week. But I've found the perspective enriching, both spiritually and financially. Like most Americans, most of my clients are conscience of, and perhaps obsessed with, Bill Gates' income and net worth. And in comparison, they usually feel very poor indeed. But those who keep the "least of these" in mind tend to feel very, very blessed. They seem happier, more content, and more pleasant to be around. They therefore tend to have more friends around the world to love. I have to believe that may also enrich them financially as they work, play, and socialize with their fellow human beings.

And as paradoxical as it seems, investing in less-fortunate nations might also enrich our own. Consider that the Japanese insisted on keeping most of their wealth within Japan during the eighties. As they invested all that money in their stocks and bonds, their markets soared. And it was fun—while it lasted. But when their securities reached astronomical levels in the early nineties, they eventually had to come back down to earth. And it hasn't been much fun since. In my view, once Japan had a sufficient amount of capital for its economy, it would have been far better off to invest some of its excess wealth in poorer nations, where the need for capital was far greater.

The same could be true of America today. Our economy is the envy of the world, and foreigners are rushing to buy our stocks and bonds due to the perceived safety of America. And the head of our central bank has spoken of the "irrational exuberance" on the part of stock market investors. Yet we keep putting the vast majority of our money into American securities. And lately we've been rushing to withdraw what money we had invested in developing nations. If we are to avoid the fate of Japan, we might begin to look at things from other than our own self-centered and/or political perspectives and try to see things from a more godlike perspective.

Elizabeth Dole often says she had to surrender her God who was "neatly compartmentalized between gardening and government." In a golden nugget, we modern stewards need to surrender our God who is neatly compartmentalized between *giving* to ourselves at church and *government bonds* for our own financial security.

In a Golden Nugget

In a golden nugget, we modern stewards need to surrender our God who is neatly compartmentalized between *giving* to ourselves at church and *government bonds* for our own financial security.

Stewardship is not simply a fundraising means of survival for mainline and Catholic churches. It is not a single-minded financial strategy for building ever larger evangelical organizations on earth. It is not Christian philanthropy for two percent of the income that our resources produce. It is not a financial perspective shaped by the spirits of fear and greed. It is not a political perspective that futilely tries to build walls around our wealth. And it is not out of touch with the economic realities of our world.

It is an enriching spirit that springs from an integrated, holistic, and godly perspective. It is a spirit for employing all of God's
resources for all of God's children. So as we approach the year 2000
and many of us begin spending more time with the book of Revelation, let's begin with chapter 3, verse 22. It says, "He who has an
ear, let him hear what the Spirit says to the churches."

Six

More Godly Perspectives for Managing Wealth

The total consecration of money to God is a prophetic act because it announces the last days. It is an element of the kingdom of heaven in the midst of us, announcing the greater and final reality of God's kingdom. It is an element of the kingdom of heaven because it means that God's grace is worth giving up everything for. But this renunciation does not mean leaving things to go their own way; it does not in any sense mean that money is given back to Mammon. It is rather a surrender into God's hands, and thus it is a reintegration. For ultimately reintegration is what lies ahead for money, when the power of money admits its submission to Christ. This is one of the last-day promises announced in both Old and New Testaments.

JACQUES ELLUL
MONEY AND POWER

I won't pretend to completely understand that mountaintop view. But if we can bring it down to earth a bit, I think the part about the reintegration of money into our religious way of life might be a most enriching thing in our age of compartmentalized morality. It is essentially remembering the vision of our Founder and using money for Christ's spiritual and material purposes—to the glory of God and in the conscious love of neighbor—rather than simply hoping our selfish pursuits will automatically prosper both us and our neighbors.

That is obviously a major challenge in a religious culture whose primary financial activity is to give two percent of our incomes, primarily to ourselves. But it might not be as impossible a task as first imagined. For it is important to notice that Professor Ellul did not envision the integration of faith and wealth management. He envisioned "*re*integration," or a return to the way things used to be before our descent into compartmentalization began after the Enlightenment. In other words, we have a rough blueprint, in historic Judeo-Christian documents, of how God might want us to manage our money.

So let's begin our journey to a more spiritually balanced life by exploring in greater detail some Judeo-Christian practices from more spiritual times. Assuming we don't swing too far back toward a purely spiritual way of life that characterizes some Eastern religions, we might pick up some ideas that might again make us truly and deeply happy as well as prosperous. And ultimately that spiritual and material balance has always been the goal of the truly abundant life, as seen from the perspective of the incarnate spiritual leader we know as Jesus.

Imagine with me that we're in ancient Egypt. The seven fat years and the seven lean ones lie immediately ahead. Our understanding of these years largely dictates our economic worldviews. Being a Christian capitalist, I believe Joseph has good intentions but is beginning to mess things up by relying on centralized planning, buying the land for Pharaoh, and making slaves of the people. If that sounds strange—and I'm sure it does—spend a few minutes with Genesis 41–47. Pay particular attention to 47:14, which says, "Joseph collected all the money that was to be found in Egypt," and to 47:21, which says, "Joseph reduced the people to servitude, from one end of Egypt to the other."

I know most Christians think Joseph was a savior figure. One of my fellow radio commentators, who is a nationally known pastor, recently told listeners that Joseph had to have been a hero because the people loved him. I respectfully disagree. People have always loved human leaders, both secular and religious, who can provide bread during rocky times. But as Malcolm Muggeridge has written, when Jesus was tempted to do so in the desert, he didn't see turning stones into bread as being his job:

> The Roman authorities distributed free bread to promote Caesar's kingdom, and Jesus could do the same to promote his. . . . Jesus had but to give a nod of agreement and he could have constructed Christendom, not on four shaky Gospels and a defeated man nailed on a Cross, but on a basis of sound socioeconomic planning and principles. . . . Every utopia could have been brought to pass, every hope have been realized and every dream been made to come true. Acclaimed, equally, in the London School of Economics and the Harvard Business School: a statue in Parliament Square, and an even bigger one on Capitol Hill and in the Red Square. . . . Instead, he turned the offer down on the ground that only God should be worshipped.[1]

I believe Jesus turned the offer down because he knew Joseph was simply another well-intentioned man who had grasped a sign of the economic times in which he lived. Like all well-intentioned men, he wanted to care for others, but as often happens, his good intentions for others turned into power over others. Notice there is no record that God ever told Joseph how to prepare for the economic cycle. There is no record that Joseph ever paid the people for their grain to start with. He only charged for it when they wanted it back. When they ran out of money, they were reduced to servitude. That story has been repeated in this old world to the days when Joseph Stalin convinced potato farmers to let him store their produce and then forced them onto collective farms. While the Judeo-Christian perspective has always seen a legitimate role for government, the story of Joseph is a good one to remember as our own well-intentioned political and religious leaders want to care for us by storing our wealth until we need it.

So I believe that the story of Joseph is one of those Bible stories that are about what we've learned not to do rather than what we should do. Since the days of Egypt, people of the Book, tradition, and Spirit have been taught, usually the hard way, that it's better to rely on God and good stewardship principles. Then we can care for ourselves and neighbors rather than rely on authority figures, either secular or religious, no matter how well-intentioned, to provide security for us.

That perspective shaped the political economy of the Hebrews once they had escaped the bondage of Egypt and established Israel. Imagine with me that we're now in that ancient land. It's an agricultural society, so we're walking through wheat fields and olive groves rather than browsing stock and mutual fund statistics. The wheat fields are square. But notice that the wheat in the corners of the fields has not been harvested. Then notice the groves where the ripe olives have been picked but the slightly ripe ones have been left hanging. Both are because Moses had said it was moral to leave part of the harvest for the poor and foreigners who were traveling through (Deut. 24:19–22). And had we been here before the harvest, we would have noticed the poor and foreigners walking through the fields and groves, helping themselves to what they needed at the moment. Yet Moses had said they couldn't carry any away in baskets, as God was equally concerned with the interests of the property owner (Deut. 23:24–25). This was an early expression of the "neighbor as yourself" way of looking at things.

As we live in an age of private property, we can't imagine someone just walking in and taking what they truly need at the moment. As we also live in an age of "efficiency," we might argue it is more reasonable to harvest the wheat in the corners and the second picking of olives. Then we would have extra for the poor. And as most care today is done through institutions rather than person to person, that extra might pay taxes for welfare or allow us to make charitable donations. Each of these may be more efficient in meeting

the *material* needs of the poor. But let's look at it from the more
spiritually balanced perspective of Moses.

He was indeed rational enough to agree that the law of supply
and demand required landowners to be good stewards who took
great care of their crops. Yet he also had the heart and soul to
understand that we and the poor and foreigners have spiritual needs
as well. He knew that in order to be truly happy people, the poor
needed the dignity of harvesting for themselves when they were
able. He would also be little surprised that we property owners find
no joy in paying taxes, and little joy in writing checks to relief organizations. And he would totally understand that the poor typically
find no joy in collecting welfare checks, foreign aid, or charity.

If we could stay in ancient Israel long enough, we might pick
up other enriching ideas. For instance, each seventh year we'd
notice that the fields wouldn't be planted or harvested. That certainly doesn't sound very efficient, but God had said it was so the
fields might restore themselves, the wild animals could sustain
themselves, and the poor and the sojourner could have plenty of
the wild crops that sprang up. And every fiftieth year we'd notice
that fields that had been bought during the previous five decades
would be returned to the original owners. That was because Moses
had said the land belonged to God, not to private individuals *or*
the government. This had the practical effect of assuring that no
family could permanently be shut out of the economy.

Of particular interest to us later, we'd discover that the Israelites
took pains to assure that their wealth did not harm their neighbors,
what we now call "social responsibility." Exodus 21:28–36 contains several good examples. Deuteronomy 22:8 urges homeowners
to be particularly conscious of our neighbors. There are many other
examples throughout the Bible.

We would also pick up some surprising ideas about the proper
role of borrowing and lending in a society. For example, it was a biblical principle to forgive all debts each seventh year. This assured that
the financial bondage of lenders would not replace the political

bondage of the Egyptians. Yet while a few conservative Christian leaders now seem to teach Shakespeare's "neither a borrow nor a lender be" as a biblical concept, Moses had a different perspective. He taught, "If there is a poor man among your brothers in any of the towns of the land that the LORD your God is giving you, do not be hardhearted or tightfisted toward your poor brother. Rather be openhanded and freely lend him whatever he needs. Be careful not to harbor this wicked thought: 'The seventh year, the year for canceling debts, is near,' so that you do not show ill will toward your needy brother and give him nothing. He may then appeal to the LORD against you, and you will be found guilty of sin" (Deut. 15:7–9). To be very clear, *not* lending was the sin.

In Matthew 5:42 Jesus echoed his words by commanding, "Do not turn away from the one who wants to borrow from you." So it is clear that both Moses and Jesus felt we should be generous lenders, particularly to those less fortunate than ourselves. And if we can see that loans among neighbors can be an enriching economic activity, perhaps we can also see that the concerns about our federal debt, eighty percent of which is essentially loans among Americans, have been somewhat exaggerated. Again, seeing things from a biblical perspective rather than a cultural or political one can enrich us in surprising ways.

Moses also said truly needy borrowers were to be forgiven their debts each seventh year (Deut. 15:1–3). Jesus said, "Even 'sinners' lend to 'sinners,' expecting to be repaid in full. But love your enemies, do good to them, and lend to them without expecting to get anything back" (Luke 6:34–35). And he taught us to pray each day that God might "forgive us our debts, as we also have forgiven our debtors" (Matt. 6:12).

From a global perspective, we should be aware that it is often estimated that each person in the Third World owes over four hundred dollars to the rich West. That doesn't sound like much, but it is more than a year's income for the 1.3 billion people we've discussed. Now think how burdened you have felt about our federal debt, which is half of our per capita annual income and eighty percent owed to ourselves. Now imagine having some despotic leader you didn't vote for, like Idi Amin, heap those debts on the backs of your children rather than having elected leaders accumulate those debts to win the Cold War against communism for our children, as our leaders did during the eighties.

In a Golden Nugget

The biblical perspective is that we, the more fortunate, should live on less than we earn so we can freely lend to others in need. We should be most hesitant to earn interest on loans to the very poorest. And we should forgive those debts if they become oppressive, rather than let them drag on decade after decade.

In a golden nugget, the biblical perspective is that we, the more fortunate, should live on less than we earn so we can freely lend to others in need. We should be most hesitant to earn interest on loans to the very poorest. And we should forgive those debts if they become oppressive, rather than let them drag on decade after decade.

That kind of lending and borrowing can enrich life in many ways. Such a biblical perspective might appear costly to lenders, at least financially in this life. But it might also assure that borrowers would not experience financial bondage and that even our enemies would know our faith through our financial activities. And that was what Jesus was truly about when he said, "The kingdom of heaven is like treasure... [or] fine pearls" (Matt. 13:44–45). How could anyone not be impressed with such a unique perspective in the money cultures of today's world? And shouldn't that really be our highest priority as stewards of God's resources? Won't it enrich us on Judgment Day?

As our visit to Israel stretches into the late Old Testament period, we find the prophets repeatedly commending the rich who cared for the poor, while condemning those who in business arrangements took advantage of—or even simply earned profits from—the poor, widows, and orphans. The prophets repeatedly cautioned against charging interest on loans to the poor. They spoke clearly concerning the spiritual dangers of riches. And they shared this perspective about how true religion might prove more benefi-cial—to both the rich and the poor—than simple religious obser-vances that we're now even broadcasting on national television: "Is not this the kind of fasting I have chosen: to loose the chains of injustice and untie the cords of the yoke, to set the oppressed free and break every yoke? Is it not to share your food with the hungry and to provide the poor wanderer with shelter—when you see the naked, to clothe him, and not to turn away from your own flesh and blood? Then your light will break forth like the dawn, and *your healing* will quickly appear" (Isa. 58:6–8, emphasis mine).

Those of us who trade our stocks and mutual funds as our cul-ture does might learn something about patience and hope from Jeremiah, who purchased a field even though he knew he would not reap crops from it for many years (Jer. 32:6–9).

If we stay in Israel until the time of Christ, we notice that mer-chants are replacing shepherds and goatherds. And money is there-fore replacing barter. While money used to be largely a long-term store of value, much as CDs are to us today, it is increasingly being used in daily life as people exchange it for what they need. So money is playing an ever more important role in the relationships between neighbors. As a means of provision, it is increasingly threatening the roles that God and love have long played in Judeo-Christian life and the love of money is therefore identified more and more as the root of considerable mischief.

The first few centuries after Christ saw three perspectives con-cerning political economy compete for the hearts and minds of those in the Mediterranean. They were the Greek perspective, the Roman perspective, and the Judeo-Christian perspective. They even-tually moved northwest into Europe and into North America to form the foundations of Western civilization. And they continue to compete for our hearts and minds today. They often get all mixed up and produce considerable political confusion and division, especially among Christians, who should be of one mind and one spirit.

The ancients basically sought to answer two questions about managing the wealth of the world. The first was, "Who owns wealth?" The second was, "Who am I responsible for in managing that wealth?" The Judeo-Christian perspective saw the answer to the first question as, "God owns all wealth." The Israelites therefore answered the second question with, "God has said I must be a good steward, as I am responsible for myself and my neighbor." This was why Moses had the authority to let the poor and foreigners walk through *God's* fields and vineyards and why no one could accuse them of stealing. It is why Jesus and his disciples could walk through the wheat fields and help themselves, even though they weren't property owners (Matt. 12:1). And because money belonged not to people but to God, Jesus could command us to forgive the loans we had made to others. Those ideas sound very strange to us, as the two other perspectives, which were once called pagan but are now called secular, now dominate our post-Christian culture.

Seeing things from what we call the "far left" end of the political spectrum, some Greeks answered the two questions quite differently. Plato may have been the first of what we now call "liberals." He answered the first question by essentially saying, "Government owns the wealth." He therefore responded to the second question with, "Government officials manage this wealth, so you have no personal responsibility for yourself or your neighbor." This is the perspective that more or less encourages "liberal Christians" like President and Mrs. Clinton to view national health care as a proper thing for our government to provide, Social Security as a positive alternative to private retirement and insurance plans, welfare as a legitimate alternative to private charity, and so on.

Yet the Romans saw things quite differently, as they looked from the "far right" end of the political spectrum. Cicero may have been the first "conservative," as he answered the first question by essentially saying, "Individuals own all wealth. It is private property." And he answered the second question by saying, "Government should simply get out of our lives so we individuals can manage this wealth as we see fit. We are responsible for ourselves." This is why "conservative Christian" economist Walter Williams has shared this perspective in *Religion and Liberty,* a conservative Christian publication: "My core belief is that we all own ourselves.... If you start with the basic premise of self-ownership, then certain absolutes of necessity follow. If it is wrong for me to take your money by force to give to a poor person, then the same is also wrong for government."[2]

This way of looking at things is also why conservative Nobel-laureate economist Milton Friedman has been quoted in the same publication as saying, "The church tends to believe that it should exercise control not only over the spiritual realm but also over the material realm, and that's where all the difficulties arise."[3] Believing that we should keep religious teachings like the Great Commandment to love our neighbors as ourselves and like the parable of the good Samaritan out of our management of material things, Dr. Friedman is often quoted for his basically Roman perspective that "our only social responsibility is to make money. Period." As I greatly respect Dr. Friedman as an economist and largely as a philosopher, I've always hoped this is one dimension of his thinking in which he's "grown."

This conservative perspective from Rome may also be why the Rev. D. James Kennedy sees this when he reads the Bible: "What does the Bible say? The Eighth Commandment of the Decalogue states, 'Thou shalt not steal.' For two thousand years theologians have been saying that this is a guarantee of private property.... The Tenth Commandment is, 'Thou shall not covet.' You should not covet anything that is your neighbor's. It belongs to him. You are not to steal it, nor even to covet it. Again, a guarantee of private property."[4]

Hence we see that well-meaning leaders on both the left and the right often espouse in our Christian media nonbiblical concepts concerning the ownership and responsibilities of wealth. They often confuse us by syncretizing pagan concepts with the most fundamental of biblical principles, such as God's ownership of everything and our management of it for our neighbor as ourselves. And this has very spiritual implications as well. For example, during the eighties I stopped thinking I owned my own wealth, and since then I haven't been nearly as angry that the government is stealing from me. That hasn't kept me from teaching the Judeo-Christian perspective that our taxes would be lower if everyone behaved themselves and we therefore needed less regulations, and that taxes would also be lower if everyone lived in charity with their neighbors. See 1 Samuel 8 for that very clear perspective.

In a Golden Nugget

As we approach a new millennium, the challenge for American Christians is to become more of one mind and one spirit by desyncretizing our Greek and Roman thoughts about managing wealth. We might then stop being "liberal Christians" and "conservative Christians" and simply get back to being Christians again.

In a golden nugget, as we approach a new millennium, the challenge for American Christians is to become more of one mind and one spirit by desyncretizing our Greek and Roman thoughts about managing wealth. We might then stop being "liberal Christians" and "conservative Christians" and simply get back to being Christians again.

If we travel with Christianity as it spreads throughout Europe in later centuries, we might find ourselves in a monastic community. It would sound strange to us to hear the monks proclaim that work is a diversion from prayer, family, and the other more important things of life. We might be startled to attend church conferences, called councils, in which our leaders are still forbidding the earning of interest, as it is considered immoral to prosper when our neighbors need to borrow something. (That teaching wasn't officially changed until about five hundred years ago, though many Jews and Christians had ignored it or figured out technical ways around it for centuries. Many theologians believe Protestant Reformers, especially John Calvin, essentially made it possible for capitalism to develop, by making it possible for the average person to earn interest on loans. Afert all, who would put money in a bank that could then lend it to businesspeople, if it was immoral to earn interest?)

One of the most influential of medieval Judeo-Christian perspectives was that of the great Jewish teacher Maimonides. Teaching around A.D. 1200, Maimonides profoundly influenced Saint Thomas Aquinas as well as leading Jews and Muslims of the period. Financially speaking, he is perhaps best known for his eight levels of tzedakah, or righteousness, with its emphasis on the dignity of each and every human being. Notice how very seriously Maimonides examined the religious life as it related to economics.

Maimonides taught that the highest degree of righteousness was to partner with a poor believer by making that person a loan or gift or by finding him or her work; the next most righteous act was to give alms to the poor in such a way that the giver didn't know to whom the alms were given, nor did the recipient know who gave them; the list continued until you got down to giving charity but complaining about doing so. (And I'm sure former president Jimmy Carter would add an even lower category, with his observation that "when it comes to charity, some people will stop at nothing," for thirty percent of Americans fit that category today.)

Quaint as all these practical concepts from history seem to us, the point is that the ancients took them very, very seriously. We moderns can learn from them by noticing that each act of true righteousness was a reflection of the spiritual relationship between God and the believer. This then inspired a loving and dignified relationship between the believer and his or her neighbors. This relationship was most righteous when it considered not only the neighbors' material welfare but their spiritual welfare as well. In essence these balanced teachings are graceful financial reflections

of the cross—vertical reflections of Jesus' command to "love the
Lord your God with all your heart and with all your soul and with
all your mind" (Matt. 22:37), and horizontal reflections of his command to "love your neighbor as yourself" (Matt. 22:39).

Each of these concepts could again help us achieve both spiritual and financial riches through the reintegration of faith and
wealth. Yet you can relax a bit. As valuable as it is to look backward
on a regular basis, the model we'll develop for the future will not
condemn anyone for making six percent returns instead of four as
happened to some Christans in colonial America. I believe that economic progress makes it possible for each generation to morally
earn a little more without losing their souls. Education, technology, global trade, and the information revolution are making it
even more possible to do so today.

A good example is how much easier it is for me to write this
book on my computer than it was for a monk to write a book by
hand during the Middle Ages. The same can be said for my publisher, who can hardly appreciate what Gutenberg had to deal with
in publishing his first Bible. Yet if reading this book enriches your
life as much as writing it has mine, I think both my publisher and
I have honored God through a moral relationship with you, the
reader who paid us for it. And though very few Christian authors
get rich by today's standards, I'm still paid handsomely compared
with medieval monks. And my publisher does well when compared
with Gutenberg.

Yet if God has blessed you richly, you may decide that pursuing
lower returns with part of your investment dollars is exactly what
God wants you to do, even if it makes no sense to today's money
culture. I essentially made that decision for part of what I was stewarding several years ago. Paradoxically, the resulting investments
have proved to be the most rewarding, in each case spiritually and
in some cases financially. Though *some* of my financial activities on

behalf of others have not been all that financially rewarding, paying attention to the ethical dimensions of my investments has kept me from losing money in other cases. The *net result* from my *total* financial activities is that I have made more money, with far greater peace of mind and joy of spirit, than when I used to invest all of it with only my personal gain in mind. I will rejoice with you if you decide to place your faith in this apparent paradox as well.

The remainder of this book is about what I believe are specific investment opportunities in the kingdom. It divides these opportunities into three categories: giving, lending, and owning. Each opportunity reflects my belief that God has provided general financial guidance throughout history, as he did with Joseph, but expects us to stay in touch through prayer, study, and the Holy Spirit, as God has also granted us considerable freedom to come up with the specifics that fit within that guidance. God is a shepherd, not a dictator. So I offer no apologies that if the specific investment suggestions in the final chapters of this book prove true, they should bring various rewards. The faithful servants in the parable of the talents enjoyed (1) the rewards of watching their productive use of resources multiply their original investments, (2) the spiritual rewards of entering into "your master's happiness," and (3) the eternal rewards of being reunited with the Master.

As our wealth is now in CDs and mutual funds rather than sheep and goats, the suggestions I offer are updated for the modern times in which we live. I believe they will bring all three types of rewards, though I know that only the last two are guaranteed. It's worth repeating that even though it's seldom acknowledged by books of this nature, the Bible still contains the story of Job, who was tested with the loss of material riches!

Each suggestion should help you see economics and personal financial management in a whole new light, one that is holistic and integrated, more like the way God may see things. A simple way of more fully understanding what I mean by that is to look at the following diagram. It explains the six ways you can look at your world, and the practical ways they can shape your finances.

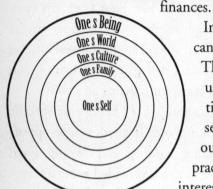

In the center of the diagram you can see a circle labeled "One's Self." That is my way of saying most of us look at most things, but particularly financial matters, from a self-centered perspective. Obviously, that is the way those who practice the "rational pursuit of self-interest" see things. But most of us do also, even if we would never admit it. As Jane Austen once said, "I have been a selfish being all my life, in practice, though not in principle."[5]

I had never realized how much my life resembled Ms. Austen's rather than Jesus', whose life tells us to deny ourselves, until very recently. That was when I looked up an old friend, the one to whom this book is dedicated. Skip was an African-American classmate when I was in grade school. He lived on the farm next to ours. As he didn't enjoy a particularly happy home life, he spent many days playing basketball at my home. (I only remember going to his home one time, and I never went in. That in itself tells me something about myself.) Skip was the best basketball player in the county and routinely gave me free lessons in the sport, as he did the other kids when we claimed the county championship.

We eventually went to the county high school, but he dropped out within weeks. He later turned up at city high, primarily because the basketball coach needed his skills. I made new friends in high school, went on to college, got married, and pursued my career. And I didn't see Skip for over a decade. But as I struggled with the decision of whether or not to go to seminary, I began to revisit my hometown, in the hope of rediscovering who I really was. And I saw Skip again. He had turned an old garage, garden hose, bucket, and sponge into a car wash.

I've tried to see Skip at least once a year since then. And we speak often on the phone. He is intrigued that the guy he knew who didn't like reading schoolbooks now writes books without anyone making him do it. And in our visits and talks together, I've learned more about who I am than I had hoped to. On my last visit I asked Skip what had happened to him at county high. He replied that he had been unable to buy meals and books and had to drop out. Strange as it may seem to most reading this book, his parents had been so angry that he couldn't manage at school on his own, they didn't let him return home. He had slept in an abandoned car by the river until the coach from city high offered him another chance at school in exchange for his basketball skills.

I've now spent several months wondering how I had attended church each Sunday and had absolutely no interest in the fact that one of my closest friends was hurting so badly. I could say, "Skip's not my responsibility; he's his parents'." And that would be *partially* true. But the only real explanation is that my self-interest was never balanced with the interests of my closest friends, much less my neighbors or even my enemies, whom Jesus commanded me to love.

During recent years I've watched the same unbalanced approach at work in the game investors play. The most obvious form of this perspective is the practice of searching for the highest-paying investments, with no regard for our neighbors, the environment, or future generations. And this is obviously the perspective of those brokers, bankers, and other professionals who are soley focused on their commissions or annual fees rather than on your investment success. Yet the unbalanced perspective shows up in many other forms as well. It is also the perspective of those many callers who increasingly ask for my counsel about mutual funds and *then* remember they don't like to pay fees or commissions to financial advisors. There's nothing wrong with doing your own homework and saving a fee or commission. But for the sake of your Christian witness to financial professionals, please do not call them about the extra money you have, ask them to help you out, and then essentially tell them you have no interest in their financial welfare!

My associates and I specialize in helping religious and ethical investors. So we often volunteer significant amounts of time and talent to helping the less fortunate, churches, charities, and so on that have financial concerns. And we are happy to do so. But we also have responsibilities to our families, charities, and so on. So like most professionals, we feel little obligation to provide free counsel to wealthy Americans. Yet we are noticing that wealthier folk in particular seem increasingly comfortable asking for our time and talents with no intent of establishing a mutually beneficial arrangement.

Perhaps it is because I am in the media myself, but I've grown to believe that this trend exists because the wealthy are most likely to read *Forbes,* the *Wall Street Journal,* and *Money* and/or listen to financial commentators. And it often seems these sources are virtually unanimous in maintaining that people are foolish to pay for investment counsel. Perhaps that is because we in the media only want people taking *our* counsel about money. So we obviously have no objections to our receiving compensation through subscription fees, advertising fees, or contributions to financial ministries. This of course simply makes the perspective we teach another of those self-centered varieties that dominate our culture.

I have long advocated reading and listening to various financial pundits. But it seems few of them feel that other financial advisors have anything to offer. This is strange. Let's use mutual funds as an example, as they are the most popular investment today. Pundits usually tell you that you should never pay a commission when buying one. They maintain that no-load funds perform just as admirably as load funds. And that's generally true, though there are certainly exceptions. Yet you do not pay commissions on load funds because they are any better than the no-load funds advertised in the media. The load doesn't even go to the mutual fund manager watching after your money. It goes to the brokers and planners counseling you about mutual funds. And their primary job is to know if you should even be in a mutual fund or not. It is only after they complete that job that they should perform their secondary function and find a manager with a sense of prudence and ethics who can deliver competitive performance.

Yet as the market has soared in recent years, it has been painful for me to hear my contemporaries in the media—who had discouraged people from investing, because of their natterings about the federal debt and so on—now look back and say that had investors avoided those natterings and been in no-load funds over the past several years, they would be as well off as if they had paid me to actually put them in funds. The reality is that my explanations of the media's near hysteria over America's financial condition during the early nineties was worth many, many times any fees or commissions investors may have paid to our firm.

Yet investors increasingly seem brainwashed by media pundits who are far better at looking back at mutual fund track records than at determining if the current state of the economy is a promising one for investors. The irony is that the *Economist* has just detailed that Americans' confidence in media commentators has declined significantly during the nineties, while their confidence in Wall Street has risen sharply.[6] So it may be time for us in the media to be a bit more graceful toward others who make a living offering investment advice. The paradox is that even if it seems to cost you a few dollars in the short run, surrounding yourself with several caring and knowledgeable advisors who can help you make sense of the world has been an enriching strategy since the days of Solomon (Prov. 12:15). Just remember that the Golden Rule suggests you should be as interested in their financial welfare as you expect them to be interested in yours (Luke 6:31).

Financial self-centeredness affects the political sphere as well. To use our old example of the federal debt, financial self-centeredness is the real perspective of those who teach that paying taxes to finance government spending is bad but earning interest from treasury and

municipal bonds that finance deficit spending by our federal and
local governments is good. Both taxes and bonds provide governments with spending money. But taxes, which finance budgeted
spending, cost us money, while bonds, which finance the deficits
and debt we say we detest, make us money. So while those who
counsel the approach may sound rather principled, they aren't really
making the philosophical case they imply. They are simply validat-
ing another self-centered ethic of our money culture that says, "If it
makes me money, it's good, and if it costs me money, it's bad." As
Congressman Barber Conable has remarked, "Hell hath no fury like
self-interest masquerading as a moral principle." Yet it always sur-
prises me how many of my fellow conservatives *preach* an admiration of business and detest government, but in their *actions*, they
keep their money in treasury and municipal bonds just because
there seems to be less personal risk there than in the stocks that
finance business.

The only way to avoid all this self-centeredness is to broaden
your perspective. So let's look at the circle on our diagram (p.110)
labeled "One's Family." Most of us have at least that wider perspective, though a few sacrifice family for personal power and
riches. But even this limited perspective can create problems. The
Mafia is an extreme example. Mafia leaders are famous not only for
looking out for themselves but for caring very greatly for their
immediate families. The problem is that their caring perspective
stops there, and they abuse neighbors in the pursuit of money and
power, though it's often rationalized as caring for the family.

So a little wider perspective would include caring for "One's
Culture," as shown on the diagram. This is the perspective that
prompted the Israelites to care for their neighbors, the poor, and the
sojourner passing through. Today it is the one that prompts many
"socially conscious" investors to avoid companies that produce
harmful products for the poor, our neighbors, and the environment.
But even this slightly wider perspective is limited, for it seems to
increasingly encourage some to build a wall around America in

order to protect what we have from others. It may be politically savvy, as most of us are self-centered enough to want to assure that our standard of living isn't threatened. And politics is usually about banding together with those of similar interests to get what we want. But as true religion is usually about people rising above their self-interest for a higher moral good—which in the long run turns out to be in their self-interest—I wonder if this political view is theologically sound, even for us conservatives.

One of the loftiest aspects of that higher moral good is the consideration of the "least of these," as Jesus put it. Since at least the days of Maimonides, theologians have maintained that the most righteous way of helping the poor of the world was to partner with them by providing the dignity of jobs. So as I've traveled Third World nations, I've often wondered why wealthy American tourists—who seem most willing to pay full price at very expensive stores—often seem to negotiate harshly with those poor folks who hand-make and market barely enough wares to keep their families fed. As I've traveled those nations, I've learned that we can grant these people more dignity, and receive far more than material objects in return, when we are as "gentle as doves" (Matt. 10:16 GNB) in our transactions, to use Jesus' words.

Yet the harsher spirit of the "serpent," to use another biblical term, has often afflicted some politicians, even religious ones, who have organized us with fear-filled techniques to keep the "least of these" subordinated to our economic interests. The most obvious example is how many of us conservative Christians subordinated African-Americans in recent centuries through the institution of slavery. We are now confessing for that sin and recognizing that it has done little to turn people into Christians. Yet I wonder if we've truly repented, as we increasingly seem to be organizing politically to accomplish similar strategies against the "least of these" in low-wage, Third World countries.

One of the most troubling and most ridiculous claims I have heard for many years is that America cannot compete with Third World nations. While it is true that they often make near-slave

wages, they have few of the competitive advantages that we enjoy—
such as the great technologies that make us the most productive
people on earth; ready access to the world's capital; convenient
transportation to the great markets of the world; and so on. To say
we can't compete with people who can barely feed themselves is the
height of self-centeredness—which is a pretty good definition of
paranoia. And it is an insult to any self-respecting American who
has taken advantage of the opportunities this country offers and
developed his or her God-given talents even minimally. Solomon
may not have lived in our "information age," but he still said in
essence, "Your education is your life." And study after study tells
us that the most direct influence on income is education. So while
there's nothing wrong with any of us opting out of the rat race that
has become our cultural norm, we should never expect our politicians to provide First World wages for Third World skills.

If you've read my previous books, you know that I've long cam-
paigned for our corporations to be more responsible about how we
treat workers. Some conservative Christian leaders are beginning to
argue the same after years of focusing on governmental shortcom-
ings. Yet I find it ironic that the same leaders are increasingly organizing us against the workers of Third World nations. As with the
slavery issue, I wonder if we may not look back a century from now
and wonder why we let the politics of self-interest blind us to our
moral responsibilities to the "least of these" once again. And as usual,
looking beyond our apparent short-term interest, we might find that
moral behavior is in our long-term interest. In *Post-Capitalist Society*, Dr. Peter Drucker has written, "The developed countries also
have a tremendous stake in the Third World. Unless there is rapid
development there—both economic and social—the developed
countries will be inundated by a human flood of Third World immi-
grants far beyond their economic or cultural capacity to absorb."[7]

I think he is correct—and may even be understating the case. Soci-
ologists tell us that absolute poverty isn't nearly as troubling to people
as relative poverty. In other words, while I grew up very poor, it didn't

bother me, as our farm was isolated and I didn't know anyone who had any more than we did. But my wife, who grew up slightly better off, felt the sting of her condition a little more sharply, as she lived in a small city with country clubs, shopping malls, and so on. So the blood shed from the Civil War to the civil rights campaign of recent years should prompt each of us to wonder what might occur when 1.3 billion people living in poverty that even I couldn't have imagined in my youth begin to watch television and see how we live in America.

So as we approach the third millennium, I would encourage an even wider perspective that considers "One's World," as seen on the diagram. This is the perspective of some, like Sir John Templeton, that it is good for all of us when the citizens of the wealthiest nation the world has ever known freely give and invest for the good of the less fortunate around the world. Yet even this perspective isn't enough, as it does neither poor nor rich much good to gain the whole world but lose their souls by simply seeing things as an internationalist rather than as a nationalist.

So beyond the perspective of one's world is another perspective, labeled on the diagram as "One's Being." It implies that how we manage God's resources is an indicator of who we are as human beings. Most Christians have long heard pastors say that our checkbooks are the most accurate biography of who we are. It is one of those simplistic techniques often used to encourage more giving to the church. But few of us have heard them say that our investment statements are equally biographical. Yet notice that the corners of the wheat field and the second picking of olives had absolutely nothing to do with the tithe. The tithe for the clergy and the poor who couldn't get to the fields was given from what was harvested, *after* the "investment portfolios" had properly considered the poor and foreigners who were capable of fending for themselves. As Moses put it, the Israelites were to do that because they too had once been poor and foreign in the land of Egypt and they should never forget what it is to be a foreigner. In other words, in every financial activity, solidarity with the poor and foreigners was a part of Israel's being, to the deepest levels of its soul. It is that solidarity that has always made us the blessed, or happy, people of God.

Finally, notice that all these perspectives are circumscribed by an endless circle of light. That is my way of saying that the ultimate dimension of wealth management transcends ourselves, our fellow Americans, our world, and even our being. Each and every decision we make about stewarding God's time, talent, and treasure has eternal consequences. For the ultimate reality of money management is that we will give a final accounting to the Master one day. I'm not sure whether that is at the end of the world at the grand final judgment or simply at the end of our individual lives, as was the case with the rich man and Lazarus (Luke 16:19–31). But it will be all too soon.

In a golden nugget, when you look at the diagram in its entirety—and understand how very short our time on this small planet truly is when measured against eternity—you are glimpsing things from the perspective of God.

It's quite a view. And it's quite a paradigm shift from looking from our own small, short-term, and self-centered perspectives as individuals, ministers, scientists, stewardship leaders, philanthropists, and investors—that is, from the humanistic perspectives. But I hope this more godly way of looking at things guides the investment opportunities found in the rest of this book. It therefore begins with a few charitable giving opportunities that I believe are particularly enriching. God knows there are many, many others that could be listed, which I simply cannot without writing an encyclopedia. So follow the spirit of each opportunity to similar organizations and strategies if that is what God wants you to do. The next

In a Golden Nugget

When you look at the diagram in its entirety—and understand how very short our time on this small planet truly is when measured against eternity—you are glimpsing things from the perspective of God.

chapters deal with the loans you can make for safety of principle and higher income to you, and those ownership opportunities that I believe may provide you with the greatest financial returns. God also knows there are some of those that I have simply missed.

While putting the opportunities for the highest financial returns last assures that you will keep reading, it also indicates that the greatest spiritual rewards you will ever receive may lie in the more immediate pages ahead. I believe these are the rewards our nation is most desperately seeking today. Yet these various ways of aiding the "least of these" in the Third World and the poor in our own country may also be the most important, as these people are the foundation of God's kingdom on earth. Our money culture is fascinated with looking at the rich and famous of the *Forbes* four hundred, *People* magazine, and so on. But I believe God has a different perspective, looking at a political economy from the bottom up.

In conclusion, I believe that the Christian perspective we need to reclaim is one that is built on paradox—the kind that prompted Jesus to say such things as "The last will be first, and the first will be last" (Matt. 20:16) and "Whoever wants to be first must be slave of all" (Mark 10:44). Though it doesn't immediately appeal to the human heart or mind, one such paradox is that investments in the poor and in our other neighbors are also good for us, both spiritually and economically. For the roof over our head is always more secure when it is built on solid foundations.

As our country was being founded, Tocqueville called that way of looking at things "self-interest rightly understood." As we approach the year 2000 and long for the country our founders hoped for, his way of looking at things could be most helpful. We just have to look at things a little differently. The ancients and our founding fathers called such a spiritually and materially balanced perspective "stewardship." As that term is no longer as rich in meaning as it once was, I'll call it "Christian capitalism," a term I picked up from Robert Schuller at the Crystal Cathedral. It is the subject of the next two chapters.

Part Two

A HOPEFUL LOOK FORWARD

Forecasters of scarcity and doom are not only invariably wrong, they think that being wrong proves them right. In 1798 [the Rev.] Thomas Robert Malthus inaugurated a grand tradition with his best-selling pamphlet on population. Malthus argued that since population tended to increase geometrically (1, 2, 4, 8 ...) and food supply to increase arithmetically (1, 2, 3, 4 ...), the starvation of Great Britain was inevitable and imminent. Almost everybody thought he was right. He was wrong. In 1865 an influential book by Stanley Jevons argued with equally good logic and equally flawed premises that Britain would run out of coal in a few short years' time. In 1914, the United States Bureau of Mines predicted that American oil reserves would last ten years. In 1939 and again in 1951, the Department of the Interior said American oil would last 13 years. Wrong, wrong, wrong and wrong again. Predictions of doom, including recent ones, have such a terrible track record that people should take them up with relish. For reasons of their own, pressure groups, journalists and fame-seekers will no doubt continue to peddle catastrophes at an undiminishing speed. These people, oddly, appear to think that having been invariably wrong in the past makes them more likely to be right in the future. The rest of us might do better to recall, when warned of the next doomsday, whatever became of the last one. Perhaps the reader thinks the tone of this article a little unforgiving. These predictions may have been spectacularly wrong, but they were well-meant. But in that case, those quoted would readily admit their error, which they do not. "The whole aim of practical politics," said H. L. Mencken, "is to keep the populace alarmed— and hence clamorous to be led to safety—by menacing it with an endless series of hobgoblins, all of them imaginary." Mencken's forecast, at least, appears to have been correct.

THE ECONOMIST
DECEMBER 20, 1997

Seven

Lend unto Others As You Would Have Them Lend unto You

> *Fixating on the Second Coming can have deleterious effects. People who think the Second Coming is imminent, scholars argue, have little incentive to worry about conditions in the here and now. . . . It is never easy to balance the hope of deliverance with a passion for the present, or the book of Revelation with the Sermon on the Mount. The greatest challenge of prophetic faith may well be to learn to pray "thy kingdom come" and then work to make it happen.*
>
> U.S. NEWS & WORLD REPORT

Several years ago a young broker read my first book, in which I explained that until about five hundred years ago the church had officially forbidden the earning of interest. He began researching the topic and discovered that the prophets had repeatedly warned against earning interest, as did church councils through the Middle Ages. He began calling almost every week. Being a self described fundamentalist, he was experiencing considerable tension from these older teachings and from the fact that he was making a comfortable living by selling bonds. These bonds were largely being bought by Christians, who would earn interest, and therefore a comfortable living, from fellow Americans, ninety percent of whom say they also believe in God. He therefore felt he was disobeying a basic biblical teaching that most of us are more comfortable pretending doesn't exist.

I don't think I've ever talked with anyone who better appreciated the spiritual and financial freedom that comes from working your way through the eye of the needle than that fine young man. I believe the graceful perspective Jesus taught in the parable of the talents and in the Golden Rule set him free of the legalisms on which his faith was built. And I believe it brought him the joy he so richly deserved for struggling with the issue. I hope it might bless you in the same way.

In the parable of the talents, Jesus had the master say these words to the unfaithful third servant: "You should have put my money on deposit with the bankers, so that when I returned I would have received it back with interest" (Matt. 25:27). From my perspective, Jesus was not simply talking about managing money. Yet I don't think he intended to exclude our stewardship of wealth from the teaching. In essence I believe he was telling the third servant that if he couldn't think of anything more creative to do with God's money than bury it in the ground, he should at least have entrusted it to someone more creative and then shared in the harvest by earning interest. That is a bit nuanced. Yet it was a more productive approach than being as absolutely certain but absolutely wrong about things as the third servant was. Without getting too philosophical, I believe that is the essence of modern banking—and therefore modern capitalism in general. Capitalism may not be the kingdom of God on earth, but it's a pretty productive approach in an imperfect world.

Yet the challenge for Christian capitalists is clearly to lend to others who will use it for truly life-enhancing activities. So this chapter is about how I've worked those nuances out in my life. You should notice that this is one of the smallest chapters in the book, as I believe lending for interest remains one of the smallest strategies for a Christian with a plan for developing the kingdom on earth. Yet there are still a few ways of lending that reflect the graceful teaching of the Golden Rule that we should do to others as we would have them do to us.

Most of us like access to capital when we have a good business opportunity. The "least of these" around the world are no different. Opportunity International is a Christian-based organization that makes that capital available. Its U.S. headquarters is in Oak Brook, Illinois, a suburb of Chicago. It is one of those organizations increasingly referred to as a "micro-enterprise" organization. That is, its mission is to create small but sustainable jobs in the Third World.

It is therefore a development organization rather than a relief organization. In other words, while relief organizations admirably provide the immediate fish that keeps a person alive, development organizations try to keep that person alive for the long run by providing the proverbial fishing pole and some fishing skills. The trick is to find those with the gumption to scout out a promising fishing hole. Opportunity International has discovered that there are millions around the world with that gumption. They just need a small amount of money for the fishing pole.

So Opportunity makes many loans of one hundred dollars to women who want to put earthen ovens or used sewing machines in their backyards. Then they can sell bread or clothes to neighbors. This allows them to work at home and care for their children at the same time. That is a terribly important thing in those regions, where most of the very poor are women and are often widows who have lost their husbands to the many ravages of the Third World. (Micro-enterprise experts prefer the term "Two-Thirds World," as it better describes the scope of the challenge.) Yet Opportunity also makes similar loans for men to buy simple pieces of equipment that allow them to make carpentry products, shoes, and other items. The big picture is that one study showed that each loan benefits up to thirteen people in the surrounding community. As many of these women and men are very entrepreneurial, they may eventually provide several jobs that impact dozens of their neighbors.

Opportunity's borrowers pay interest on their loans. Yet that doesn't mean the wealthy in America, Australia, Europe, and so on who provide the money are profiting at the expense of the very poor.

They are donors who are not expecting return of principle or interest but are simply trying to gracefully give back as they've been given to. However, an increasing amount of money is coming from institutions making "soft loans" to the micro-enterprise organizations. This means these institutions wouldn't mind getting their principle and a low rate of interest back someday, but it won't bother them a great deal if they don't. In that sense it's like many loans between family members. Only it's a very large and very extended family! God's family!

Most of these donors and lenders simply want to get money more directly to the poor than has happened when foreign aid has been given to governments in the Two-Thirds World. This is how Opportunity helps that happen: It has regional coordinators in Africa, Eastern Europe, and so on. Their job is to find the local Christian businesspeople who will lend their business and professional skills as volunteer board members. Working with them, Opportunity hires and trains staff members who work directly with the poor entrepreneurs. Ultimately these not-for-profit, indigenous organizations may become autonomous, self-supporting entities.

The money is loaned so that when the borrower prospers, he or she can repay it and it can be used to help yet another poor person. The interest pays some of the overhead of making the loans and offsets some of the currency devaluations that are a normal part of business in these areas. The repayment rate is a rather remarkable ninety-five percent, far higher than the rate at which our college students repay loans. We find that this is because access to affordable credit is a treasure that people in the Two-Thirds World protect.

Another reason why the repayment rate is so high is that Opportunity often employs a group-lending concept known as a "trust bank." This means borrowers are often partnered with other borrowers in a particular "bank." They trade with each other, learn business principles from each other, and encourage each other to repay their loans so others will have capital too. You—or your church, your civic club, and so on—can fund such a trust bank for about thirty borrowers, with a gift of ten thousand dollars. From your trust bank, you'll receive regular reports describing how your gift is changing lives in remarkable ways. You will be blessed.

While no one claims that micro-enterprise organizations are perfect, I believe they are so much closer to the biblical concept of lending to the very poor with no expectation of interest or return of principle that I have served on Opportunity's board for several years and now chair its finance committee. There are other advisors you may better recognize, like Millard Fuller of Habitat for Humanity, Bob Seiple of World Vision, author and sociologist Tony Campolo, and religious historian Martin Marty. Some donors appreciate the fact that Opportunity International has an affiliated Women's Opportunity Fund with its own board and staff. You may request additional information about either by calling 1.800.7WE.WILL. We accept any amount of contribution. But if you are going to give only a few dollars a year—and we're most appreciative of that—you might request that you be put on our minimal mailing schedule, as we can use up quite a bit of your donation by staying in touch more than you want. As we can change a life for one hundred dollars in the Two-Thirds World, we want all the "mites" possible getting to those who live on little more than faith.

———————————

People often ask if Opportunity makes loans in the United States. We have experimented with that idea. But it's been rather difficult to create a job here for a couple hundred dollars, or even for a few thousand dollars. So I've found another organization that I believe is better suited for spreading a little Christian grace here at home.

It is called the South Shore Bank and it is located in Chicago, though it now has branches and affiliates in several areas. Probably the best-known of the "community development banks," it was partially financed by churches when it was established. The primary reason why the churches got involved was that they didn't think the old joke about only being able to borrow money from a bank if you don't really need it was all that funny. Community development banks, and the often poor people they serve, don't think it's so funny, either. So while many banks collect deposits in poorer areas and ship the money to wealthier, up-and-coming areas, community development banks reverse the process, as they believe life can be enriched in poorer neighborhoods, neighborhoods that might soon add to our urban problems if neglected.

While many banks lend our deposits to credit card borrowers and such, South Shore specializes in making construction and mortgage loans, primarily to people who want to rehabilitate and own affordable private housing. This does several things to reverse the condition of deteriorating neighborhoods. It provides jobs in high unemployment areas. It therefore turns welfare recipients into taxpayers and shoppers. That allows local merchants to prosper. It also provides affordable non-project-style housing that people want to own. And the cycle of destruction stops. In essence it is not unlike Henry Ford's idea that if people made enough money building cars, they would have the money to buy cars. The more cars they bought, the more they would get to build. And so on. But it takes the creative spark of the entrepreneur to set the cycle in motion. And as usual, that spark is often ignited when the heart, mind, and soul cross signals.

At one time people scoffed at the idea of cars being an economic opportunity. And people often do the same when I tell them about the opportunities in America's inner cities. Yet an article on the editorial page of the *Wall Street Journal* has suggested that retailers should consider a huge "growth frontier right in their own backyards—America's inner cities.... Inner-city markets are attractive because they are large and densely populated. Despite lower household income, inner-city areas concentrate more buying power into a square mile than many affluent suburbs do. But they are badly underserved, often lacking the types of stores that inundate suburban areas." The *Journal* estimated the spending power of our inner cities at $85 billion a year, which is more than the spending power of Mexico, America's third-largest trading partner after Canada and Japan.[1]

Yet community development banking is not a purely economic activity, as is the case with my local bank, where I also keep a few dollars. In essence South Shore is another financial institution that resists the growing trend toward the simple rational pursuit of self-interest (merely paying the highest rates to be found) and the worship of efficiency (like that efficient but soulless practice of banking by Internet). By employing heart and soul, South Shore keeps a touch of humanity and grace in our financial lives. I find that brings back memories of a time when life seemed richer in some ways.

I remember that when I was in college, I would occasionally bounce a check. My hometown banker would honor it, call my parents with the news that I had done it again, and they would stop by the bank as soon as it was convenient. As they knew everyone in the bank, they would chat a bit, probably laughing that a college student headed for a career in financial services couldn't balance his checkbook. I miss that bit of small-town life every once in a while as I efficiently zip into my local megabank, punch the buttons of my automatic teller, and zip on without talking to a soul.

So I keep my son's college savings in South Shore for the balance it offers. Every once in a while I drop by the bank and talk with some new friends I've made there. That's not to say South Shore operates entirely from the heart. It pays rates on my son's CD that are every bit as competitive as I get at my efficiency-driven local bank. Deposits receive the same FDIC insurance, though I doubt it will ever be needed, as South Shore is well managed. In fact, it seems to hang around, while my local bank has been merged once again. It offers most every type of checking, certificate of deposit, and retirement plan you can think of. You can get information on any of its programs by calling 1.800.NOW.SSBK. As you read it, notice that you too will get what I call the "triple bottom line" of a financial return, the social return of being a part of the solution to America's most pressing problems, and the spiritual return of knowing you're a reflection of God's grace. (As a disclaimer, you should know that I began serving as the advisor to the bank's retirement plan a couple of years back and could indirectly benefit a small amount if you help them grow.)

_____

When Sherry and I were first married, we were most grateful that someone was willing to loan us enough money to buy our first home. And having a reasonable mortgage proved both financially and spiritually more enriching than renting year after year. So now that we and our retired clients have a little extra ourselves, we try to finance mortgages for others. We do that by buying government-guaranteed securities called Ginnie Maes.

In essence, when you borrow money from a bank, savings and loan, or mortgage company and make your monthly payment, it may not end up at the institution from which you borrowed the money. Many institutions today originate your loan but then package it with other loans and sell them to investors. If the lending institution gets the loans backed by a government agency called the Government National Mortgage Association, or GNMA, before the loan package is sold to these investors, the bonds have the guarantee of our federal government. And they are conveniently called Ginnie Maes, after the government agency that insures them.

Ginnie Maes are very popular with conservative investors, for several reasons. First, they typically pay about three-quarters of one percent more than U.S. treasury bonds. Second, they also pay monthly interest checks rather than the semiannual checks that treasury bonds do. Finally, some of my more socially conscious investors, and especially politically conservative investors, appreciate the fact that they finance housing rather than the deficit spending of our federal government, as treasury bonds and E-bonds do.

As with any—repeat, *any*—investment, there is a negative side to Ginnie Maes. The first negative is that Ginnie Maes return a part of your principle each month, as mortgage payments are part principle and part interest. This means you need to be careful not to spend everything you receive, or you'll eventually run out of money.

The second negative is that new Ginnie Maes sell for a minimum of twenty-five thousand dollars. While you can buy an older Ginnie Mae, which has returned part of its principle over the years, for less, the minimum can still be higher than many of us have for one particular investment. The final negative is that Ginnie Maes fluctuate in value from the time you buy them until they mature. So you shouldn't invest short-term money in them. As a general rule, I don't invest money that I or my clients might need in less than five years.

Many investors like to purchase Ginnie Maes through a mutual fund, as that can eliminate some of the negatives listed above. All Ginnie Mae funds that I know of reinvest your principle before sending on your monthly interest check. So you don't have to worry about running out of money. And most have far lower minimum investments. In addition, purchasing through a fund allows you to switch to other funds within your mutual fund family if your needs change over the years. As it can often cost five percent to buy and then sell a Ginnie Mae in increments of less than one hundred thousand dollars, the ability to switch to other funds can be a major advantage should you want a different investment. Yet the value of a Ginnie Mae fund can still fluctuate, so plan to hold on for five years or more. And your income is not quite as steady as with a single Ginnie Mae. Funds contain many differing Ginnie Maes that come and go over the years, thus changing the income somewhat as interest rates change.

Most mutual fund companies have Ginnie Mae funds. If you don't work with any particular fund company, you can research possibilities in the independent mutual fund service called *Morn ingstar.* It can usually be found in your public library. Or the two largest Ginnie Mae funds might be a good place for you to start. While large size can hinder the performance of some stock funds, it can be something of an advantage for Ginnie Mae funds. This is because large funds generally buy the bonds more cheaply and have lower expenses. Of these two funds, one is offered through investment brokers and one is marketed directly to the public.

The Franklin U.S. Government Securities Fund is a load fund offered through brokers, meaning you typically pay a commission when you buy it. That hasn't kept it from becoming the largest in the country, containing almost ten billion dollars as I write. In its most recent report, *Morningstar* says this about the fund: "The fund has earned those assets with three, five and ten year returns in the category's top quintile, and with risk scores in the tamest. What's more, the fund's payout has been near the top of the category for the entire decade. Lead manager Jack Lemein's long tenure, along with Franklin's solid record of managing fixed-income funds, add to this fund's appeal."[2]

Minimum investment is only one hundred dollars. See your broker or call 1.800.342.5236. While you can order the fund directly from Franklin without a broker's help, you still pay a commission. However, retirement plans, endowment funds, foundations, and wealthy individuals with larger amounts to invest can often purchase the fund without a commission. Ask your broker or planner or see the prospectus for details.

The second-largest fund in the country is the Vanguard Fixed-Income Securities GNMA Fund. It is marketed directly to the public, meaning you don't pay a commission to buy it. At present it contains a little over eight billion dollars in assets. Its risk rating is slightly higher than Franklin's, but its return has been slightly higher as well. *Morningstar* says this: "This fund's incredible record is founded on two basic tenets. The first is that over any significant time period, low expenses will have a positive impact on its relative returns. The second is not to make bets that are so large that, if they prove incorrect, they will overwhelm the fund's expense advantage.... Manager Paul Kaplan certainly isn't in danger of violating the second rule [but] that isn't to say that Kaplan never makes bets."[3]

Minimum investment is three thousand dollars. You can order a prospectus by calling 1.800.662.7447. Though I've often wondered why Vanguard believes you should pay a manager to watch over simple government bonds but not riskier stocks, Mr. Kaplan has made enough good decisions that I often recommend the fund.

Back in the eighties and early nineties I recommended a lot of treasury bonds to clients. Our federal government was borrowing a lot of money for defense spending for the Cold War. My parents and grandparents had bought a lot of war bonds for "hot wars" like World War I and World War II. And I thought it was an equally legitimate use of money to lend some to our government to win this particular war, which thankfully didn't require the use of bullets as much as economic policy to win. (I believe history will show that the huge deficits of the eighties were due to this defense buildup and that the more recent balanced budget was due to the Cold War ending. Yet like the rooster who thinks the sun comes up after he crows, our very human politicians like to claim credit for now balancing the budget. But reality may be that the march of God's history toward freedom for humanity played a significantly greater role.)

Many people stopped buying government bonds a few years back, as they thought we had entered a period of low interest rates. It surely seemed so, as our perspectives were shaped by the thirty-year treasury bond paying thirteen percent during the early eighties. But a little longer perspective, which is another spiritual principle, suggests otherwise. The thirty-year treasury bond paid only two percent when I was born in 1950. It didn't pay over four percent until 1965. It was only when the Vietnam War began that inflation, and consequently interest rates, began to soar. (Again, during war our government must either tax us more heavily for guns, which is most unpopular, or it must borrow money and/or print money. Borrowing money runs up the federal debt, as happened in the eighties with the Cold War. Printing it runs up the inflation rate, as happened in the seventies during the Vietnam War. Either eventually pushes interest rates higher than they would normally be. So one of the blessings of today's peace is your lower mortgage rate!)

I've noticed recently that almost no one is taking my advice to buy some bonds as well as stocks. The response is, "Why buy bonds paying six to seven percent when I can buy stocks making twenty percent?" The answer of course is that stocks don't always make twenty percent, despite what you are now hearing from many media sources, including ministries.

Some of my wealthier clients like to buy tax-free municipal bonds. And I don't totally discourage them. Some clients need the stable income that municipal bonds offer. And municipal bonds are typically loans to local and state governments that want to build airports, hospitals, and so on, so it can be a good use of money. Yet I've never thought they made particular financial sense for younger investors, even if these investors are in their peak earning years and paying high taxes. Even they can normally pay the taxes on their stock gains and still have more money left than if they buy tax-free bonds.

For example, assume you pay twenty percent capital gains taxes on the gains from a good stock fund. If you make the twelve percent historic returns that American blue-chip and foreign stocks have delivered since I was in high school in 1968, you would still have over nine percent after-tax returns. That is considerably higher than what tax-free bonds are returning. Still, if you believe the stock markets are somewhat inflated and vulnerable to a correction— and I do today—it could be good for you and our country to shift a little money into municipal bonds.

Municipal bonds normally come in increments of five thousand dollars. If you can't buy at least five different bonds for diversification, I'd suggest you consider a good mutual fund that invests in municipal bonds. Again, if you don't know too much about municipal bond funds, you might be well served to start with the two fund houses that manage the most munis. And coincidentally, they are Franklin and Vanguard, so you again have a choice of using a broker or saving a commission by doing it yourself.

The largest muni fund at Franklin is called the Federal Tax-Free Income Fund. It contains over $7 billion. *Morningstar* says it produces "above average" returns with "below average" risk, and summarizes its advice with: "This offering looks like a top choice for conservative, yield-hungry investors."[4] Minimum investment is one hundred dollars. See your broker or call 1.800.342.5236.

The largest muni fund at Vanguard is called the Municipal Intermediate-Term Fund. It contains almost $7 billion. *Morningstar* says it produces "average" returns with "below average" risk and summarizes by saying, "Despite the fund's stumble this year, its history of strong performance and risk control, as well as rock-bottom fees, should go a long way toward assuaging any fears investors have."[5] Minimum investment is three thousand dollars. Call 1.800.662.7447.

People often ask me about corporate bonds, both investment-grade or high-quality, and non-investment-grade or "junk" bonds. I've never been a particular fan of either. Part of the reason is philosophical. I don't believe in debt on my business. So I don't lend much to businesses that do. The other part, however, is practical. If I want to finance a high-quality company, I'd rather do it by buying its stock rather than by buying its bonds. Decades of history have shown that stocks produce higher returns than bonds do. And if a younger or lower-quality company wants me to finance its operations, I'd just as soon do it by buying some of the stock—the same stock that is normally owned by the people who started the company or now manage it. (Have you ever heard of any executive working for options on the company's bonds or putting money in a bond purchase plan?) If you disagree, however, *Morningstar* covers plenty of corporate bond funds.

I know all this probably seems like a strange way of looking at your investing. Your view has long been shaped by banks, brokers representing corporations, and others who want to borrow your money and pay you some interest. And they usually only want you to consider what these investments will do for you, rather than what they will do for your culture, your world, and your children. Further, you have probably never heard anyone in the church suggest that God might still think that it is enriching for us Christians to steward the world's wealth by buying stocks rather than loaning our money to others so they can own and therefore manage that wealth as they see fit. Yet study after study tells us that God's upside-down way of looking at stewardship has been far more rewarding than the way governments, banks, and corporations have asked us to look at it. And owning and managing the world's wealth in a "responsible to God and neighbor" way is the subject of our next chapter.

Eight

Creating Riches for Your Neighbor As Yourself

You don't have to believe in Armageddon to need reminding that we live in a world where a lot of things can go wrong. Salvation, however, does not lie in Swiss francs, or gold bars. It lies in a middle path between blind optimism and blind panic.

FORBES

Imagine the rest of your financial life as a journey. It is a journey between the two ditches of fear and greed. You have to choose four things for this journey in order to travel the "middle path" to "salvation." First, you must choose the route that you want to travel. Then you must choose the vehicle you wish to travel in. Then you must choose how you will maintain the equipment on that vehicle. Finally, you must choose where that journey will end, with riches in this world and/or riches in the next.

Some of us like our roads to be scenic interstate highways with few bumps or curves. And we like our cars to be what my eleven-year-old son Garrett calls a "floater," meaning a big Cadillac or Buick. Then we can turn on the cruise control and some soft music and proceed to glide on down the road, barely thinking about our driving. We are the investors who put all our money into certificates of deposit and treasury bills. Then we never have to be concerned with any of those dips and curves in the stock, bond, and real estate markets.

Smooth, straight, and scenic interstates are wonderful things. But they do have their problems. The biggest is that all by themselves, they can rarely get you where you want to go. If you want to get to some destination, you almost always have to first travel two-lane highways or city streets, which have more curves and bumps. Similarly, history tells us that stocks, bonds, and real estate may have some curves and bumps, but they are good for getting us to a point where we can cruise along with only a few T-bills and CDs as we grow older.

On the other end of the spectrum are those of us who like some fun in our driving. So we buy small, quick sports cars and head out for the back roads. We scout a map of the general direction we plan to travel and we put the pedal to the metal, as the truckers like to say. We are those speculators who study financial newsletters about what gurus believe the economy and markets ahead will be. We then place our bets on risky penny stocks and junk bonds to take quick advantage of anticipated smooth roads, on gold coins to protect against any rocky roads, and on options and futures for the dips in between. And we enjoy the excitement. Yet we quickly discover that no map can tell us about the fallen trees, road construction, and many potholes in the road ahead. After a time of this, and particularly after a crash, the smooth ride and safety of the floaters on the interstates can look pretty good again. So we trade in our speculations for safe investments. But time passes, we forget about the crash, and we eventually look for a back road again.

Despite common perceptions, we don't always need help from investment professionals to trade roads and vehicles far too often. For example, one major study from Dalbar that has been quoted for years showed that those who bought no-load mutual funds without the assistance of a professional trade them twice as fast as those who buy load funds through brokers. And not too long ago I wrote for a Christian financial newsletter that recommended the trading of no-load mutual funds at a far faster clip than any broker I have known.

More recently Terrance Odean, a professor at the University of California–Davis, has completed a review of ten thousand accounts

at a major discount brokerage firm, where investors are not chauf-
feured by a broker. He concluded, "Investors are too cocky and
don't know as much as they think they do . . . they should trade less
and take a buy-and-hold approach."[1] His review actually showed
that the stocks investors sold outperformed the ones they bought
by an average of three percent over the next year. Over the next two
years, once transaction costs were included, the investors were over
nine percent worse off than had they simply done nothing. His
advice was to "stop looking at the financial news every day. And
don't trade on the Internet. It's too easy."[2] (Remember my talking
in the introduction about the paradox of doing less and making
more money as a result?)

What you really want is a vehicle that you can be comfortable in
for the long haul. Sort of a sport utility vehicle, or SUV. While it
too can get banged up some in a crash, it is more dependable than
most of the other vehicles, on most any kind of road. SUVs are relatively comfortable on the interstates, manage winding roads fairly
well, and are one of the best things you can be in when the road
turns rocky. And SUVs are about the only thing you want to be in
if you want to get to the top of a mountain so you can enjoy a very
rare view. This versatility and dependability is primarily due to the
SUV's four-wheel independent suspension. In effect this means one
wheel can hit a pothole that might stop the floaters and sports cars,
and the other three wheels keep us moving toward our goal.

The same is true of an investment portfolio that might help
you avoid the fate of seventy percent of Americans who get to
retirement without sufficient savings to continue their lifestyles. It
too needs to be properly balanced in four basic areas. One of the
wheels on the front might be short-term investments, like certificates of deposit and treasury bills, that serve as emergency money.
The second wheel on the front might be bonds for the stable
income they provide year after year as short-term interest rates
bounce around and CDs and T-bills no longer provide the income

we need. Together these two wheels offer *control* for those times in life when the stock and real estate markets throw us a curve.

The wheels on the back aren't for control but for *powering* us to our destination. So one wheel might be the ownership of domestic stocks and real estate that prosper us when business conditions are smooth in the United States. And the fourth wheel might be international investments that prosper us when our markets hit a pothole but things are going more smoothly around the world.

The other reason why SUVs are all-purpose is the four-wheel-drive option. In essence, while the front wheels normally provide control and the rear wheels provide power, the front wheels can begin to pull when times get particularly rough. Similarly, CDs and Ginnie Maes give us control but rarely the pulling power of stocks and real estate when the economy is smooth. But when the economy grows rocky, such as in a serious recession or even a depression, they can provide some much needed control in protecting our purchasing power.

While a four-wheel-drive SUV would seem to be an ideal vehicle, some of my clients still prefer more unusual vehicles. A very few even prefer a unicycle, meaning they like the simplicity of having their money in one place—even if it means there's an increased likelihood that they'll topple over if they hit a pothole. For example, I remember when many retirees thought a unicycle was a good approach when short-term CDs paid double-digit interest rates. They kept all their savings in them, thinking they were safe. Yet their incomes crashed when interest rates dropped. And many had to invade their principal in order to live. There's hardly anything safe about spending your principal.

Others might like the slightly more complicated motorcycle approach, meaning they put half their money in income investments, such as bonds, and half in growth investments, such as stocks. There's a good possibility that this approach will get you where you want to go. The danger is that you'll get bumped around pretty good when inflation worsens. Adding a few short-term CDs and real estate, which benefit from higher inflation as stocks and bonds suffer, can again smooth your ride.

Yet some investors like to go to the other extreme and insist on an eighteen-wheel truck to carry them and their money around. In other words, they believe you can never have enough investments. That's a somewhat valid approach, assuming you don't mind the constant maintenance of keeping up with all the tires. Yet even if you don't mind all the statements, annual reports, and tax accounting, you should still make sure that all the tires aren't exactly the same. In other words, I often find that investors own eighteen mutual funds but that each fund is invested in blue-chip stocks, or each fund is invested in government bonds. That is almost exactly like riding a unicycle. If stocks or government bonds should hit a pothole, all your wheels will bounce you around as if you only had one tire on your truck.

Forbes magazine once asked Sir John Templeton how many funds the typical investor should own. He replied, "If you own a fund that can invest without restriction in at least 100 different stocks and bonds worldwide, then one fund is sufficient diversification. Even for very large investors with many millions to invest, nothing is gained by owning more than three such funds. You've achieved maximum diversification. The whole thing is a matter of common sense, but I suppose that's why it's not common."[3]

A more likely explanation is that few financial publications or advisors could earn a living by saying, "Buy one to three good funds and leave them alone." Things have to be considerably more complicated in order to keep you reading or calling month after month. Yet I can assure you that one of Sir John's best friends has, on Sir John's advice, invested principally in two global funds for many years to complement his real estate and bank deposits, and I know few investors who have done better.

———————————

Investors should never focus their sights on the rearview mirror. But my twenty years on Wall Street, and even a longer study of economic history, tells me the SUV is a pretty good approach for most of us. And that's especially true for those of us who are humble enough to admit that we don't know about the potholes and other obstacles that may lie in the road ahead. For example, when I started in the investment business in the late seventies, most Americans thought they couldn't lose money in real estate, due to the inflationary road ahead. Stocks were getting bumped around and bonds were being deflated as interest rates set new speed records. But it wasn't long before the road took a turn and inflation slowed. Real estate suffered a blowout and stocks and bonds raced on to smoother times. On the international front, oil-producing companies in nations like Mexico rolled during the late seventies when oil prices soared. But the stocks of oil-consuming nations like the United States dropped off small cliffs for the same reason. When oil prices later hit a bump, the opposite occurred.

If you were smart enough to anticipate all those curves and bumps in the road ahead, you could have made a fortune. Thousands of wrecked savings and loans, real estate limited partnerships, energy companies, penny stock firms, and junk bond houses at home, and Asian investment banks abroad, attest that many of our brightest financial experts weren't smart enough to see them coming.

While we will never know the exact road ahead, we can always see some rather simple items that can smooth the ride. For example, it is a fairly simple task to check the pressure in the tires every once in a while. If one is low on air, it can slow our progress. Yet if it is too inflated, it can burst as it becomes too hot at high rates of speed. The same principle applies to investing. In the early nineties there were some relatively simple checks that said the air in our stock market was too low. A major reason why many of us couldn't see that was because we were intently staring in the rearview mirror at that pothole America had hit that was called the federal budget deficit. Yet while hitting a pothole can make a tire go low on air, it doesn't necessarily mean it is ruined. In fact, if it is a high-quality tire, it can still have many miles left in it.

So I encouraged people to add some air (money) to the stock market tire. Yet in the past three years we have added so much that U.S. stocks have gone up twenty percent per year. That hasn't happened in over a century. Some of that air was needed. But what we've added in the past year or so probably hasn't been. Ben Graham, perhaps the most disciplined stock analyst of all time, called the stock market "a highly illogical place where sheeplike investors follow the flock and buy when prices rise and just as mindlessly sell when prices fall." I don't think that's the kind of sheep Jesus wanted us to be. In other words, many investors have been adding air to that tire just because others have been. Yet that's just when an explosion, and possibly a crash, is most likely. So I'm now suggesting it might be wise to let a little air out of our domestic stock holdings by taking a few profits. And I'm putting air in other tires that have hit potholes lately, like the once hot but now nearly deflated Asian stocks.

Again, please notice that this has nothing to do with my predicting potholes in the road ahead for U.S. stocks. They are surely there, to challenge *all* our tires. I simply believe it is futile to try to anticipate them, especially now that the world's markets are moving faster and faster. Trying to be godlike and see beyond the immediate road ahead simply distracts me from the humanly possible matters like checking the air in the tires. Yet while I hope our U.S. stock market continues to roll along just fine, the various gauges we use to check the pressure tell me that it is more than fully inflated. (Listen carefully and you'll notice that the pundits who advocate putting more air into U.S. stocks are not looking at the gauges but are seeing the road ahead as perfectly smooth.)

No one really knows how high these gauges can go before the tire bursts. That depends on several unknown variables. The economic road ahead might turn out to be perfectly smooth for the first time since Abraham set out on his journey. Investor sentiment toward our stocks might cool and the market could drift sideways, also keeping it from bursting. Or these same sentiments might overheat and add even more pressure to the tire, making an explosion even more likely. No one—but *no one*—can predict such things. But you don't really need to in order to read the gauges and keep your tires within the safe range.

What we call the "price/earnings ratio" or "P/E ratio" of the Dow Jones Industrial Average is probably the most popular of the stock market gauges. And it is as high as we've ever seen it at this stage of the economic cycle. Another popular but less reliable gauge is the amount of dividends (quarterly checks) our corporations are paying out to stockholders in relation to stock prices. It has never been as far into the red zone during the twentieth century.

A less well-known but more accurate gauge is called the "q-ratio." And it too is far into the red zone. Very simply, the q-ratio is the one you get if you compare the stock and bond values of our corporations with the corporations' replacement values. The replacement value is the estimate of what it would cost to replace the factories, equipment, and so on at *today's prices*. (The more popular "book value" is the price the corporations *originally* paid for those items. But that grows irrelevant with the passing of time, with inflation, and so on.) The market valuations today are twice the estimated replacement values, meaning the q-ratio is nearing two.

In essence this is similar to paying two hundred thousand dollars for an existing home when you could build it for one hundred thousand dollars. Most of the time, the stocks and bonds representing the value of existing corporations are like the prices of existing homes. They have to be discounted slightly below replacement values in order to be sold. So there has only been one other time in its relatively short history that the q-ratio has risen slightly above one. That was in 1968. And stock market investors lost about seventy-five percent of their purchasing power during the next six years.

Yet none of this seems to bother American investors. In 1997, Americans placed a *net* $240 billion, or 2.6 percent of America's gross domestic product, into stock mutual funds. To put that into perspective, that's almost $100 billion more than we gave to all charities last year. (We only give about $75 billion to all religious causes.) And that's not bond funds, money market funds, real estate investment trusts, or individual stocks. Just stock mutual funds.

While I certainly have nothing against stock mutual funds, it might be a good time to wonder if God will honor such financial imbalance in our lives. (In previous books, I've suggested we balance our *total* investing with our charitable giving.) From the 1930s through the 1980s we had averaged investing under .5 percent of GDP into stock mutual funds. The only time we have seen anything nearly similar to today's enthusiasm for these funds was in 1929, when we invested 1.5 percent of GDP. And we know what happened then. So it could be worth remembering that a financial publication printed these words in August 1929: "The establishment of mutual funds by banks and independent groups has almost become a fad. The public appetite for them grows even more rapidly than the funds can. They represent buying power in the stock market that appears to be without a saturation point."[4]

It's also worth noting that stock mutual funds have historically kept between five and fifteen percent of their money in cash equivalents in order to buy stocks during a dip. In recent months these cash reserves have been at record low levels. This could indicate they won't be able to support the market should it begin falling.

So what is the proper amount of air for the front and rear tires of your portfolio? That depends on the road you want to travel and how fast you want to go. But for the average driver, one good rule of thumb is to treat your age as a percentage and put it in the two tires up front. In other words, if you are forty years old, put forty percent of your assets into government-guaranteed investments like CDs from South Shore Bank and Ginnie Maes. Then put the other sixty percent in those wheels on the back, or the nonguaranteed domestic stocks, real estate, and international investments. If you are sixty years old, you would reverse that.

Notice two very important points about using this particular gauge. First, when you are younger, you will have more in the investments in the rear tires. They have the best track record of providing the powerful growth of purchasing power that you may need when you retire. Conversely, as you grow older, you will put more and more money into the more conservative, guaranteed investments of the front two tires. They can then steer you around the obstacles that markets experience. This formula assures that you will grow more conservative as you grow older. By the time you are eighty, for example, you will have only twenty percent of your money subject to the potholes and curves of the stock, real estate, and international markets. Some of my senior clients say even that is too high. But having counseled Florida retirees for quite a while, I can assure you that those celebrating their one hundredth birthdays are increasingly common. Who knows what advances in health care might mean for all of us? And inflation can decimate a portfolio in the twenty years between age eighty and one hundred.

Second, notice that as one tire grows overinflated, there will normally be a tire that is lower on air that you can add to. For example, as I edit this book in the summer of 1998, Asian stocks have hit a very deep pothole, just as Mexican stocks did back in 1994. But our bonds are soaring as investors from all over the world are seeking safety from the crash. So as the pressure in the bond tire has risen higher, it might be wise for true long-term investors to begin puffing more air in the now lower international stock tire that might allocate some money to Asian stocks.

I know that's extremely difficult to do. Just as our bonds did in the early eighties, our stocks did in 1987, our real estate did in the mid-eighties, and so on, the Asian pothole gave investors a jarring experience. But that's precisely the time you need to add air. (Surely you've heard that the Mexican stock market rose fifty-five percent in 1997? No? That's a good indication of how our media focuses on the negative!) Tires rarely go low on air when they've experienced nothing but smooth roads. If you avoid adding to them when they are low, your only alternative is to add to tires that are already properly inflated or possibly too inflated. And it's simply more enriching when you buy low than when you buy high. That means you have to buy after potholes have been hit.

One of the only ways I've been able to do that over time has been to treat my investments as if they were charitable donations. We seldom give money to those who have been experiencing smooth roads. We give to those who have hit a pothole of life. It's a basic principle of the religious life—and it can enrich our investing as well as our giving. But again, it means we can't have these two financial activities in separate compartments of our thinking.

————————————

How much air do you need to keep adding to assure you will get where you want to go in life? Again, that depends on your destination. If you're driving for a simple retirement, modest savings should suffice. If you're heading for *Forbes'* list of the four hundred richest people in America, you'll need to save considerably more. But I like two gauges for most people. The first is what I call the "10-20-40-500" plan. If you can earn *ten* percent on your money, which is the historic norm for the U.S. stock market, can save *twenty* dollars per week, can work *forty* years before retiring, you'll have a nest egg of *five hundred* thousand dollars.

The second gauge is for those who may be a few years into their career and haven't started saving. They might subtract twenty from their age and save that percentage of their incomes. In other words, if you haven't started saving and are forty, you need to start saving twenty percent of your income. If you are fifty, you need to start saving thirty percent, and so on. Both gauges are rather imprecise as you have to adjust them for your own style of driving and destination. But they are reasonably sure to keep you between the ditches of fear and greed.

I've described the South Shore Bank CDs, Ginnie Maes, and municipal bonds I believe you might consider for the front of your car. The following are some ideas you might consider for the rear.

It is not an exhaustive list, and there could be others you should consider. But I have three criteria for mentioning them. First, they are professionally managed investments, as I believe you are wise to hire a chauffeur unless you are a very experienced driver. I know that the smooth roads of the past fifteen years have left many of us thinking we're ready for the Indianapolis 500, but I'm unconvinced. (And even after fifty years of terrific stock picking, Sir John now manages his personal money largely by buying mutual funds.)

Next, these professionals specialize in conservative investments and conservative strategies. If you accept my thesis that markets today are moving so fast that very few of us can steer around the potholes, you want to have very high quality tires. Then they can withstand the occasional bumps and keep going. Second, they have a history of ethics. I believe we have entered an age in which the rule of the financial road is: If it makes money, it's good, and if it doesn't make money, it's bad. So it's a particularly good time for Christians, and only common sense, to have their money with professionals who have proved there are some things they'd prefer not to do for money. Finally, this combination of prudence and ethics should have produced solid returns for several years. None of these three criteria of prudence, ethics, and past performance offers any guarantees during a crash, as do the CDs and Ginnie Maes. But they have taken a lot of people where they wanted to go over the decades.

For that domestic stock tire on the rear of our SUV portfolio, the American Funds group out of Brea, California, has a couple of very popular funds that have packed a lot of power over the years. Its Washington Mutual Investors Fund is a favorite among many churches, foundations, and individual investors. It now contains almost $35 billion and is one of the very largest stock funds in the country. *Morningstar* rates its risk as "below average,"[5] as it invests in only the bluest of blue-chip companies. And it generally avoids the sin stocks of alcohol, tobacco, and gambling companies, as well as short-term trading. Yet it has averaged almost twenty percent annualized returns during the bull market of the past fifteen years.

American Mutual is a sister fund to Washington Mutual and now contains almost $10 billion. It is considered more conservative than Washington, as it will normally contain a few more bonds and money market instruments. It has similar prudence and a similar ethic yet has averaged over seventeen percent per year during the past fifteen years. Both Washington and American are normally load funds offered through brokers, or you can call 1.800.421.4120 for a prospectus. Minimum investment is $250.

The Pioneer Group of funds also drives rather prudently. Its flagship Pioneer Fund has a "below average" risk rating.[6] And it is the oldest mutual fund in the country that has generally avoided the sin stocks. Yet had you put twenty dollars per week into this fund since its inception in 1928, your investment of about seventy thousand dollars would be worth over seventy *million* dollars today! That's a remarkable fourteen percent average annual return during seven decades, beginning with the Great Depression and including several wars, lots of inflation, and many recessions. And it is clear evidence that your investments do not have to violate your sense of prudence and ethics in order to prosper. The Pioneer Capital Growth Fund is also worth a look, as is their Emerging Markets Fund. Again, they are normally load funds, so see your broker or call 1.800.225.6292. Minimum investment is $1,000.

The Domini Social Equity Fund is one stock index fund that doesn't think intelligent investing means disconnecting the heart. It avoids the sin stocks, weapons manufacturers (or "defense companies," for us conservatives!), and nuclear power companies. About half the companies in the Standard & Poor's 500 make it into this fund. *Morningstar* says that its risk is "average" but that it has produced "above average"[7] returns of over twenty percent per year over the past five years, which is about how long it has been around. It is based on the Domini 400 Social Index, which has just outperformed the Standard & Poor's 500 Index for the third consecutive year, again proving that socially conscious investors can do well for themselves by doing good for their neighbors. It is a no-load fund, and you can obtain a prospectus by calling 1.800.762.6814. Minimum investment is $1,000.

The Pax World Fund has a "low" risk rating,[8] as it's a "balanced" fund that normally keeps a sixty-forty blend of stocks and bonds. In addition to the sin stocks, it also avoids weapons manufacturers, so it's a longtime favorite of many pacifists. It has averaged over fourteen percent annualized returns over the past fifteen years. It is a no-load fund, so you must call 1.800.767.1729 for a prospectus. Minimum investment is $250.

There are three newer funds that have been introduced in recent years that you might also look into. The first is from the Mennonites and is called the Praxis Growth Fund. (*Praxis* is a theological term meaning the intersection of faith and practice.) *Morningstar* has given the fund one of its top two ratings.[9] It has two companion funds, a bond fund and an international stock fund as well. They are load funds and are distributed through a select group of brokers nationwide. You may also call 1.800.977.2947 for details. Minimum investment is $500.

The second is the Neuberger and Berman Socially Responsive Fund. It has an "average" risk rating and is the most aggressive domestic stock fund I'd recommend to you. It has an "above average" rating for return.[10] As it invests primarily in medium-sized companies, it's a good complement to the funds I've listed above, for those willing to take slightly higher risks. It is a no-load fund, and you can obtain a prospectus by calling 1.800.877.9700. Minimum investment is $1,000.

And the last is the Citizen's Emerging Growth Fund. It has rather extensive social screening and a short but promising track record. You can call 1.800.223.7010. Minimum investment is $2,500.

There are two other funds that I'm often asked about that I can't recommend but that you may wish to explore on your own if you are an aggressive investor. The first is the Parnassus Fund. It is a volatile offering that has an "above average" risk rating, and it can hurt you in a down market.[11] But it has also averaged over twenty-two percent a year during the past five years. It is a low-load fund, and you may call 1.800.999.3505 if you are interested.

The other fund is called the Timothy Plan, which was developed with extensive social screening that might appeal to conservative Christians. It had a slow start but has recently changed managers and seems to be doing better. Yet most of the holdings are small companies, and you should expect some volatility if the economy grows bumpier. It is a load fund, but you can obtain a prospectus by calling 1.800.TIM.PLAN.

You may also wish to complement your domestic stock holdings with some real estate. I have three favorite ways of doing that. If you want a conservative, income-producing investment and plan to hold on to it for several years, you might take a look at the Corporate Property Associates (CPA) series of real estate investment trusts. These are essentially mutual funds of large corporate properties. Each pays a tax-advantaged quarterly income that is normally very competitive with bonds. Yet they tend to benefit from inflation, as their income is indexed to the inflation rate. So the higher the inflation rate, the higher your income. And inflation often makes real estate values rise as well. So they are a good complement to domestic stocks and bonds, which can suffer due to higher inflation rates. I've used them since the early eighties, and they made money for my clients when many real estate investments didn't. You may call 1.800.WPCAREY for a prospectus on the most recent offering. The older units have merged and now trade—at a premium to investors' original cost—on the New York Stock Exchange under the symbol CDC. Minimum investment in the new program is $2,500.

If you need more liquidity, or the ability to sell your holdings quickly, you might consider the Cohen & Steers Realty Shares. It is a no-load mutual fund that invests in several different real estate investment trusts. These REITs are typically more aggressive than CPA's REITs and only pay about half the income that CPA's REITs do. But you'll have added diversification, and you can get your

money in and out more quickly. Minimum investment is $10,000.
Call 1.800.437.9912 for a prospectus. If you don't have that high
minimum, you might consider the Franklin Real Estate Fund. It is
a load fund but has averaged similar returns during recent years
and allows $100 minimum investments. Call 1.800.342.5236.

The final wheel on our vehicle would be international. While
most Americans believe it's a relatively new phenomenon for one
nation to help other nations through investments, the *Economist*
has shared this enlightening look in the rearview mirror: "Despite
the newfound popularity of international investing, capital markets were by some measures more integrated at the start of this century than they are now. During the thirty years before the first
world war, huge sums flooded from Western Europe into North
America, Argentina and Australia. The net outflow of capital from
Britain averaged five percent of its national income during those
years. In comparison, Japan's notorious outflow has averaged only
two to three percent over the past decade."[12]

There are several reasons why I believe international investing
continues to make sense as we approach the new millennium. The
first is simply that diversification generally enhances safety, assuming you do it right. While many of us believe America contains
most of the large, safe companies on earth, the reality is that the
investment firm of Morgan Stanley has estimated that the ten
largest construction and housing companies are outside our bor-
ders, as are the ten largest real estate companies, seven of the ten
largest automobile companies, and seven of the ten largest chemi-
cal companies as well.

International markets also offer significant growth. During
1997 the respected Ibbotson Associates estimated that international
markets had outperformed blue-chip American stocks since 1968.
So much of the strength we've seen in our markets in the past five
years is simply us catching up to their previous superior performance. (Though much of our comparative advantage has also been
due to the weakness in Japan's market.) Morgan Stanley has even

estimated that in the past twenty years the United States has *never* been the top-performing stock market in the world.

In addition, international stock markets do not all move in the same direction or to the same degree as our market from year to year. Investors call this mirroring of our market "correlation." For example, the Bloomberg advisory service has just estimated Canada's correlation with our market as being .62, meaning its fluctuations only mirror our market's by about sixty-two percent. Great Britain's correlation was estimated at .41; Germany was .37; Chile was .15; and Turkey was a minus .02, meaning it goes in the opposite direction as ours. So it is clear that international diversification can help smooth the road.

Yet as I edit this book, Asia has been the latest market to hit a pothole and has therefore dominated our headlines. Many of my clients are feeling they should simply bring all their money home. (Again, most of us make our driving decisions *after* we've hit the pothole, and therefore also tend to move our money to the tire that is already the most inflated!) Few Americans realize that the *Wall Street Journal* has written a major article that states that the Asian tire may be low on air but still looks pretty strong. "As Asia stumbles from one economic crisis to the next, a vital truth is often overlooked: Most Asian economies continue to grow at speeds that, by the rest of the world's standards, are remarkable."[13] And the *Economist* essentially said that although riding on four wheels may increase your odds of hitting a pothole, it doesn't mean it is smarter to begin riding on one wheel. "Last week investors who had bought shares in different countries lost money everywhere. That does not alter the case for diversification.... Last week's global crash should not sound the death knell for international diversification. Although the world's stock markets mostly fell, the degree of correlation should not be overstated. Some markets dropped much further than others. And some rebounded quickly while others did not.... The occasional crash aside, there has been no great increase in correlation between stock markets in different countries for several decades."[14]

I like the following international investments for prudence, ethics, and performance. Several of my favorites are from the Templeton Group of funds. In fact, when clients tell me they have to ride a unicycle for some reason and can only buy one mutual fund—which I don't recommend—I usually put them in the Templeton Growth Fund. The reason why is that while all mutual funds aren't really *an* investment as much as a *portfolio* of investments, this one is particularly so. It normally contains over two hundred different high-quality stocks and bonds from many of the nations of the world. And it is an "unlimited" fund, meaning it can invest in whatever the manager believes is the most promising stock or bond at the moment. In essence it is a bit like saying you don't want to drive or perform routine maintenance, so you would like the Templeton people to do both.

Most of the time, the fund is heavily invested in international stocks, though it was predominantly in U.S. stocks in the early nineties. Proving its conservative nature, it was over thirty percent invested in bonds in the early seventies when stocks all over the world had become too expensive and were being deflated. This conservative approach has been so rewarding that *Morningstar* gives the fund a "low" risk rating but a "high" return rating.[15] It has averaged over sixteen percent during the past fifteen years and generally avoids the sin stocks as well as short-term trading.

If I thought the U.S. stock market was so inflated that I didn't want any money invested here and only wanted international stocks, I'd choose the Templeton Foreign Fund. It is a sister fund to the Growth Fund and is very similar, except that it doesn't have roughly twenty-five percent of its money in U.S. stocks. It even has the same manager, Mark Holowesko. *Morningstar* gives the fund its top rating and says its risk rating is "low" and its return is "above average."[16] *Mutual Funds* magazine recently seconded the opinion by saying, "Foreign is a consistent peer beater, topping our international index nine of the last ten years, all while exposing its shareholders to less than average risk. . . . Portfolio manager Mark

Holowesko has overseen all but four months of that stellar performance, and has doubled the returns of his peers during his tenure. . . . Concerned about market volatility? Templeton Foreign earns an 'A' down market rank. The superior rating reflects the tendency of international markets to move independently of the U.S. and Holowesko's value philosophy."[17]

Studies indicate that a thirty percent allocation of your stock portfolio to the major nations of the world may produce greater returns with lower risk for conservative investors. Yet more aggressive investors might consider putting about one-third of that, or about ten percent of their total portfolios, into the developing or emerging nations of the world, especially now that those fast-moving markets have hit a pothole. Again, I look to the Templeton organization for that. Few of us may believe it after the past *five* years, but over the past *ten* years the Templeton Emerging Markets Fund, the oldest emerging markets fund, is *still* outperforming our S&P 500.[18]

But you might consider the Templeton Developing Markets Trust. *Morningstar's* most recent report said, "This fund is still the champion of its category." And the *Wall Street Journal's* magazine called *Smart Money* recently said, "No one's done a better job of investing in the emerging markets than manager Mark Mobius. Over the past five years, his Templeton Developing Markets Trust has compounded at almost sixteen percent per annum, several points ahead" of the second-best fund.[19] Minimum investment in all Templeton funds is $100. They are normally load funds offered through brokers, but you can obtain a prospectus by calling 1.800.292.9293.

The *Smart Money* article concerning investing in the emerging markets was about funds that "have done a better job than others of dodging the disasters and making the most of the good times."[20] Other than the Templeton Developing Markets Trust, the magazine only found one fund that had done so. It was the Pioneer Emerging Markets Fund. It is a smaller fund than the Templeton fund, which allows it to explore some smaller nations and companies of the world. So it could be a good complement to Templeton. Minimum investment is $1,000, and it is a load fund offered by brokers. Or you can order a prospectus by calling 1.800.225.6292.

There may be a few readers who need to better manage the taxes that the investments above might generate. That gets beyond the scope of this book, but such readers should simply know that each investment may be utilized within an IRA or other retirement plan. Many of these investments have also been "cloned" within "variable annuities" for those who need to defer considerable taxes until retirement, and "variable life contracts" to pass assets on to children while avoiding federal income tax. Please consult with your investment and/or tax advisor to see if those approaches might be appropriate for your particular needs.

At this point you are equipped with a basic Christian way of looking at things, a Christian spirit that eliminates the fear and greed that drives the human heart, and a pretty good idea of how to integrate both with your financial life. The only question remaining is basically whether you will or not. It is not an easy question for American Christians.

Since the late eighties I have had many, many people tell me that when they've read my books and asked their advisors about my ideas, they've been steered in other directions. So as we approach the year 2000, even they believe in the concepts but practice others. In other words, if anything, American Christians are even more compartmentalized in their thinking; are continuing to worship money from Monday to Saturday and God on Sunday; are increasingly blessed by the priests in the secular temples of Wall Street and Washington who like it that way; and are baptized by religious leaders who don't know the differences in the religions.

Yet your decision remains the greatest risk-reward calculation you will ever attempt. I would like to tell you that it is a decision that will change this old world. I'm not sure it will. There's certainly a case to be made that Wall Street and Washington tend to give us what we want and that if the ninety percent of us who say we believe in God truly believed that the "root of all evil" hasn't changed over the millennia, they would give us more love for neighbor rather than more love of money. But I expect that the rewards of your decision will be more personal, reflecting these words from Henri Nouwen, a great theologian and human being who died not long ago. He once taught in the great seminaries of Harvard, Yale, and Notre Dame and probably thought he might one day change the world, too. But he later grew closer to the truth when he moved to a community of disabled people, where he could simply love neighbors in need. And after doing so, he wrote, "God rejoices. Not because the problems of the world have been solved, not because all human pain and suffering have come to an end, or because thousands of people have been converted and are now praising him for his goodness. No, God rejoices because *one* of his children who was lost has now been found."[21]

The end, however we define it, may indeed be near, and the reason why I know that is because Jesus told us to always be ready and alert. But when it comes to our relationship to money and wealth, we risk losing our souls if we yield to the secular perspectives that tempt us to ignore the Christian perspective that one's journey here is simply a school for the spirit. As the following appendix about Y2K that I've added as we go to press indicates, ministries continue to prompt fear and anxiety over the future, regardless of what the Lord said on the mount. So as we approach the third millennium, it is my more fervent prayer than ever that your end-times investments of money, time, and talents will bring peace to your soul, adequate prosperity to your future, and much rejoicing by our Lord.

Appendix: Y2K

Armageddon, Opportunity, or Hype?

> *The millennium stirs America's strong religious instincts. Pre-millennial tension has been said to agitate cults and militia groups. Things as unconnected as the so-called Hale-Bopp suicides and the Oklahoma bombing have been blamed on zero-based date fever. Yet this surely is confusion. As the millennium ends, people across the world are anxious about all sorts of looming catastrophes, probable or improbable. Only a handful of calendar nuts are seriously worried.*
>
> THE ECONOMIST
> APRIL 18, 1998

I love to immerse myself in the deeper perspectives of a well-written book. So I've never learned to "surf the Net." My best friend is a busy executive who lives by email. But his voice tells me how he's really faring in his hectic life. So when he feels there's something we need to share, I insist he slow down and call me. The ministries I serve know that if they want to reach me in a timely fashion, they had better send a letter by "snail mail," as I read my emails about once a month. All this is a way of saying that you are *not* about to read a "techie's" perspective of the Y2K problem. For my fellow nontechies, Y2K is the potential problem looming on January 1, 2000, when some computers adopt our attitude and refuse to completely adapt to the new century.

In fact, I almost never wrote this chapter at all. I added it near the very end of the editing process as more and more clients began talking about Y2K. Personally, I'd never thought it important enough, in this grand drama we call life, to worry about. As Jesus assured us on the mount, if it truly threatens our food, drink, or clothing, there will be plenty of pagans worrying about it enough for all of us.

I thought this issue was like the federal debt, which I totally ignored in my first book. I wrote it in 1990, and none of the truly thoughtful people I knew or had read thought it was a "crisis." But I quickly learned that if you're going to help conservative Christians, you'd better address the perspectives we pick up from our media. For, with notable exceptions like Robert Schuller's *Hours of Power* and a few other free bearers of "Good" news, the media has enough time to fill with programming that it can worry us silly about every dimension of life. So for the past several years I've wasted considerable time trying to overcome what the *Economist* once termed a "paranoia that has become an American habit." And frankly, that was valuable time that I could have spent educating more people about more ways to enrich themselves both spiritually and financially by enriching their neighbors.

Some very thoughtful Christians I know have that perspective of the Y2K problem. For example, I go to church with a dear friend who until recently was the chairman of one of the world's most technologically advanced major companies. It is increasingly involved in integrating information you'd normally get on your computer with what you can get on your television. He calls that "convergence." And he thinks convergence will play a major role in educating your children one day soon. As his company is betting tens of millions that computers will continue working, I feel he knows what he's talking about.

He's also the son of a mainline minister and serves on the board of one of America's best-known megachurches. So he understands the Christian perspective. And when I asked him how the Y2K problem would affect us, he calmly replied that industry and government have been working on the problem for years. He feels the odds are good that the vast majority of us will wake up in the next millennium and wonder what all the fuss was about. Yet he believes there will undoubtedly be some isolated problems.

As those problems might affect some of the money I steward for myself and my clients, it was only prudent that I brush up on the various perspectives of those handful of folk who do worry about such secular matters. But frankly, having been immersed in the eternal dimensions of life—as deeply explained in that well-written book we call the Bible—during the several months I've spent writing this book, I'm still far more interested in the spiritual dimension of the issue than in the Internet's chatter. For as the quote from the *Economist* at the beginning of this appendix indicates, the way religious folk look at world events seriously affects how our neighbors look at religion. And it doesn't help for them to see us as a handful of nuts. So the most important thing I'd share is that I'd much rather lose some of my money than for all of us to lose our souls.

Yet all Christians apparently haven't learned to appreciate that biblical perspective just yet. For example, in August 1998 Pat Robertson devoted his 700 Club to the Y2K problem. It promoted a free special report on how the church might begin to respond. (If you're interested, the report is available by calling 1.800.945.5879.) The show featured Pat, Larry Burkett of Christian Financial Concepts, and Joel Belz of *World* magazine. They seemed most concerned that even at this late date, the church has not begun to respond. And they seemed unaware that some Christians have explored the problem and decided there's nothing to respond to.

The show had been promoted in my local paper as a look at the Y2K "crisis." So I expected its perspective to be similar to the ones the 700 Club shared about the savings and loan crisis, the crisis in the Middle East, the federal budget crisis, the Social Security crisis, and the other normal problems of daily life. And the show did use the word *crisis* repeatedly. In fact, I don't remember anyone ever describing Y2K as a "problem." One pastor actually suggested that the couch potatoes watching needed to adopt a "crisis mentality" in order to effectively address the problem. And I noticed that at the end of the show, a promo described the next day's show about yet another crisis about to hit a major area of America. So I wondered which crisis viewers should worry about first. And I realized why many Christians are described as having "compassion fatigue," even while our giving to benevolences, as opposed to our giving to ministries like the 700 Club, grows smaller and smaller.

As this book goes to press, the *Economist* has graciously provided an update of Y2K in a special eighteen-page report. It concluded,

> The greatest worry about the Year 2000 *problem* may be neither its potential impact on economic growth, nor, probably, its potential impact on human welfare. Rather, it may be the extra uncertainty it will create just at the moment when the world economy is already becoming increasingly fragile, with confidence shaken by events in Asia and Russia, and weakened by the faltering of America's long boom. Since the start of modern times, the end of a century has been a time of economic unease. The British and Dutch stockmarkets in 1699 and 1799 and the Dow in 1899 all saw sharp falls in prices.... Between December 2nd and 18th 1899, the Dow fell by 23%. A millennium, even more than a centennial, would be spooky enough without the fear of computer failure. *Perceptions, rather than reality, may turn out to be the most dangerous aspect of that pesky millennium bug.*[1]

And of particular interest to this book, the *Economist* report commented on the ironic problems that end-times expectations can create if the future should unexpectedly happen:

The computer was invented at just the wrong time. Had it been developed before the first world war, say, or in the past decade, the point of distinguishing between dates in different computers would have been obvious. But the computer was born smack in the middle of the century, *when some people thought humanity might never see another millennium.* The first two digits of the year seemed dispensable.[2]

There were some rays of hope that occasionally broke through in the 700 Club special. The celebrities took pains to suggest we avoid "radical" solutions to the problem this time. Near the middle there was a clip of Ron Blue—another Christian author who often appears in the media—admitting that the bunker mentality is the biggest problem among conservative Christians. That was encouraging. For many years the show's celebrities have routinely ignored the brightest economists and financiers of Wall Street as they've encourage millions of Christians to seek shelter from the financial storms and earthquakes they've forecast. They've kept many of my clients from prospering in the past seven fat years. They've sent many Christians packing to other lands in order to protect "their" resources. So while I was tempted to dismiss this as another case of them crying wolf, I tried to remember that despite his very earned lack of credibility, the little boy did eventually warn of a real wolf— and no one listened.

The show acknowledged the common wisdom that Wall Street firms have run extensive tests on their computers and have found no problems. I found that amazing, as in twenty years on the Street, I've rarely had a day when some mutual fund company, insurance company, or bank hasn't told me its computers are down and I'll have to call back later! Which is an important point. It's guaranteed that some computers, ATMs, and so on will develop routine problems on January 1, 2000. You can expect that those media pundits who've predicted a crisis will point to each one as validation of his or her warnings that the sky is falling.

But we should hesitate to allow such normal challenges of life to deepen our pessimistic worldview. For example, Larry Burkett ended the special by saying he has an oil company credit card that expires in the year 2000 and it won't work already. As merchants routinely tell me they accept the same kind of card each day, my guess is the oil company is simply pestering Larry because of his attitude toward credit cards! Seriously, as the old saying goes, two anecdotes, much less one, don't constitute a scientific study. Nor should one malfunctioning ATM prompt a bank run reminiscent of 1929!

But some of their advice was also very reasonable, and I'd suggest you follow it—assuming you don't already. For example, they suggested that if you normally keep a week's worth of cash on hand, you might keep a few weeks' worth as we approach the new year—just be aware that if everyone takes more than a few weeks' worth, we'll probably have a banking crisis! (The Federal Reserve is already printing extra cash for that eventuality). They suggested that if you have funds in banks and securities firms, you might keep hard copies of your statements rather than rely entirely on their computers. As if I've ever had a client who did otherwise.

Outside the financial arena, they suggested you avoid flying on January 1, 2000. As if anyone could drag us away from our football games. They suggested you lay in a few weeks' worth of food in case the railroads don't work. I normally have that many leftovers from the football games. And even that is often wasted, as I'm trying to "fast" my way back into my clothes. Now there's a wonderful opportunity to turn lemons into lemonade! And they suggested that those of you who live in cold climates might lay in some firewood in case the electricity goes off for a few days. My mother lives in Kentucky and has done that for years. But I'm keeping our spare bedroom in Florida available just in case she gets caught up in millennial fever and forgets! So don't call, as the room is already booked.

In short, if you want to survive this latest "crisis," it seems you should basically do a few commonsense things that millions of us around the Caribbean have done for years each time a hurricane approaches—yet I've never heard a hurricane described as a "crisis."

Just as I have for many years when listening to these celebrities, I found myself wondering about that missing perspective of Jesus—that only "the pagans" worry about where their food, drink, and clothing will come from. Yet this time there was another major biblical perspective that they insisted in not only ignoring but actually refuting. It is the same one conservative Christianity tends to gloss over in many dimensions of life. It is the one about the root of all evil.

At the very beginning of the show, Pat devoted about seven seconds of the one-hour special to explaining that some experts think the "crisis" is simply hype from computer consultants pursuing a quick buck. Yet it was clear that Pat didn't think that could be the root of this particular evil. So he immediately conducted a live interview with Peter de Jager, the leading consultant and prophet of doom surrounding Y2K. He has made some interesting and helpful points in recent years and did so again. But I thought the special might have had a more balanced perspective had Pat also interviewed Dr. Paul Kedrosky. For only days earlier he had written these words in the *Wall Street Journal,* beneath the headline "To Figure Out Y2K Hype, Follow the Money":

> Remember the cartoon "Pinky and the Brain"? Every week, two talking mice created elegant, simple and completely unworkable plans for world domination. . . . The Year 2000 *Problem* is like a lost "Pinky and the Brain" episode, with the media warning that a tiny computer glitch could cause big problems. . . . The media spotlight has people in a tizzy from the fringes to the financial center. On the Internet, survivalists are busy giving advice on how to stock your bomb shelter for

when the power goes off. At the same time, Deutsche Bank's gloomy chief economist, Edward Yardeni, said Y2K is likely to cause a global recession. [Note: I found that interesting, as Ed and I worked for the same Wall Street firm during the eighties. We had nicknamed him "Doom and Gloom Yardeni." We learned to ignore him as the stock market soared. Eventually he moved to his new firm, where he now dispenses gloomy perspectives of the millennium and as much of our world is now in near depression, forcasting the possibility of a recession is hardly a prophetic act!]

It is easy to see why the story has gotten as much attention as it has. Combine millennium anxiety with a simple-to-describe technology problem and then mix in our fascination with all things computer-related, and you have a story tailor-made for the evening news. It may be a recent media discovery, but the Y2K story itself is an old one. Programmers and industry experts have known about the *problem* for years, since at least the mid-1980's. While many public and private organizations have been lamentably slow in acting on that knowledge, fixing the problem is well under way at most organizations. . . . So if real progress is being made, then why is the Y2K drumbeat getting louder rather than quieter?

Chalk it up, in part, to millennial madness, and also to disaster being a better story. But there is another dimension to the story, one best found, as always, by following the money. Who wins financially if Y2K remains a big problem? The answer: consultants, software vendors and lawyers. An unholy alliance of companies all see the Y2K problem as a money-making opportunity. Peter de Jager not only speaks and sells books on the problem, but has collaborated with the American Stock Exchange on an index of Year 2000 companies. There is, of course, nothing wrong with making money by solving problems, but it is hard not to be a little suspicious of all the self-serving doom and gloom.[3]

All the self-serving doom and gloom may enrich not only unholy companies but an unholy media selling only a fearful perspective. When the July 1998 issue of *Money* explored Y2K, it quoted three experts. They ranged from a pessimist, who was Ed Yardeni, to a realist from the Federal Reserve Board, to an optimist, who was Ed Kerschner, chief investment strategist of Paine Webber, who said that Y2K "fears are overblown." I wondered why our Christian media couldn't find a realist or optimist to interview.

And I wondered why Wall Street, for all its problems, year in and year out seems a greater source of hope—one of the Big Three of faith, hope, and charity—than does a substantial part of the conservative Christian media. For example, only a week before the 700 Club special counted our Y2K problems, a major Wall Street firm issued a special report whose headline claimed that Y2K could be a "blessing in disguise." Right or wrong, it said,

> Thanks, in part, to the prophecies of Y2K alarmists, the syllables now conjure up as many visions of a countdown to Armageddon as the seemingly unexciting, albeit labor-intensive, chore of finding ways to add two digits to year-related dates ... [but] the simple premise behind the "blessing in disguise" interpretation is that companies around the world will use the Y2K challenge as an opportunity to upgrade or replace systems altogether, employing the newest available technology, which will create a widespread increase in efficiencies—all of which helps not only the individual companies but, potentially, works to help keep inflation levels in check, too.... With the Y2K issue, we try to look at the difference between perception and reality. Some observers have ignored it as a nonevent, while others have preached doom-and-gloom. In all likelihood, the real consequences will lie somewhere in

between the two views—although we wonder sometimes whether paranoia might overwhelm common sense.[4]

As if to dispel any doubt, within a day of the 700 Club special someone told me about a local pastor who plans to remove all his money from his bank and investment firms until Y2K is over. The irony is that if all the Master's sheep follow this particular shepherd, our economy is guaranteed to plunge off a cliff. And the pastor will probably congratulate himself for anticipating the great need of those who have fallen on hard times.

And we shouldn't assume Wall Street is simply being Pollyannaish. All the truly informed people hardly agree the problem must become a crisis. When I told a friend I was writing this chapter, he sent the August 1998 issue of *Wired* magazine. It does feature some computer programmers who see it as a crisis but also acknowledges there are differing perspectives. It said, "If heightened technical awareness alone could explain the apocalyptic conclusions drawn by the Y2K survivalists, then every well-informed geek would be moving to the desert—and that clearly isn't happening. . . . Ultimately, it all comes down to faith."[5]

So it should be of particular interest to those of us who go from year to year trying to discern Christian prophecy from cultural paranoia that *Wired* then observed, "Throughout history, prophets and visionaries have spent their lives preparing for the end of the world. But this time veteran software programmers are blazing the millennial trail. The geeks have read the future, not in the Book of Revelation, but in a few million lines of computer code."[6]

It is surely ironic when people of faith who read the Bible have the same worldview as secularists who read computer code—or federal budgets or all the other things "the pagans" worry about.

And *Wired* noted other ironies in Y2K. In the early nineties it seemed that every doom-and-gloomer was convinced the federal debt would sink the economy. Yet they inevitably advised us to put most of our money into treasury bonds, which are loans to that very same supposedly bankrupt federal government! But *Wired* noted that this time around, many doom-and-gloomers are "heading for the hills," a line the 700 Club used in promoting its special. Yet *Wired* concluded a sidebar entitled "The Great Blackout of '00" by saying that the possibility of blackouts in small regional power companies, which was a topic of considerable discussion in the 700 Club special, "suggests an ironic scenario: Remote areas may remain dark for weeks or months after January 1, 2000, leaving Y2K survivalists waiting in their isolated cabins for the lights to come back on— while complacent urban dwellers enjoy uninterrupted service."[7]

Perhaps most ironic, and most sad, *Wired* described Paloma O'Riley, who runs a popular Y2K Web site. And it specifically contrasted her with "the militia types and fundamentalist Christians."[8] Interestingly, *Money* magazine called this week, and it too seemed to think those two phrases go together like "bread and butter." So I was intrigued that as many militia types and Christian fundamentalists head for the hills—and according to *Wired* are laying up more firepower than I had in the army, at least until I moved to the field artillery!—Paloma O'Riley is staying put, as "when she looks around her community, she doesn't see potential looters—she sees neighbors." It described her as a "firm *believer* in the notion that some good, old-fashioned community-building may keep the Y2K nightmare at bay." And it concluded, "Her worst-case scenarios look much the same as those of the most hard-core, self-sufficient Y2K survivalists, but the bomb-shelter aspect is conspicuously missing. Paloma *believes* that people will pull together in times of turmoil."[9] Though I have no idea if Paloma is a Christian, I admired the two parts about belief.

I was also saddened when Pat interviewed several pastors who are ready to capitalize on the gloom. Some actually said that Y2K will be "a once-in-a-lifetime opportunity." Their theory is that when things get bad, more Americans will approach their churches for help or consolation, and they can evangelize them. Having served on church boards, I can assure you that had my pastor ever made such a comment, I'd suggest he or she take a very long sabbatical. For those pastors desperately need to spend a few months working with Habitat for Humanity, Opportunity International, or the many other Christian organizations that have found opportunities available each day for decades to help people whose lives have crashed and who are too busy surviving to worry about a computer crash.

Another well-intentioned pastor showed a storeroom where his church had laid in enough food for the church's members and "a meal or two" for the several thousand people of his community. He acknowledged that even the pastors in his community think he's a bit nuts. And as I looked at this storage room, I realized it didn't contain nearly the food the typical cruise ship stores each day. I couldn't help reflecting on how much smaller some of us in the church today think than did Joseph when he planned seven years in advance to store up enough provisions for the crisis of Egypt. And I wondered if we wouldn't be more relevant to our culture if people thought they'd be better off in one of our churches than on a Y2K-compliant cruise ship celebrating a new millennium. Surely we would be if we noticed that the Two-Thirds World is hurting today and little concerned about the computers of the next millennium.

I think that small, self-centered way of looking at our world was the part about the special that, again, saddened me the most. As one *friendly* author has noted, our small, crisis mentality truly has become "the scandal of the evangelical mind." For when Joel Belz was asked how Christians—at least the conservative ones he knows—see the Y2K problem, he said he had brought two items that summarize their perspectives. The first was a can of sterno. It symbolized those who were storing up emergency fuel, rations, and so on in case there truly is a crisis. And the second symbol was a gun. A real gun! He said some conservative Christians were stockpiling food and guns with the intention of shooting anyone who tries to take their food.

I now have a disturbing vision of Christians lying in dark cabins on January 1, 2000, using guns to protect their hoarded supplies from other survivalists who have been in the hills too long. With their dying breaths, they exclaim they were right after all.

Meanwhile fifty miles away others are mildly annoyed at delays at banks, grocery stores, and gas stations.

While Joel never referenced the current fad for "What Would Jesus Do?" bracelets, I was heartened that he at least rejected hoarding food and guns in the hills as a valid Christian response. But I had to wonder why he didn't also question storing up emergency fuel and supplies. For like most Americans, I was watching in the hopes of finding some way to keep my stove working. And we are surely left with some unanswered questions.

To return to our football analogy, now that our media personalities have stopped hunkering down in the locker room beneath the stadium, is it enough for us to simply sit in the stands praying for our team to begin losing? Economically, America is the winningest team in the history of the world. Industry and government have been on the field a long time during this economic expansion. They've been gaining ground against problems like Y2K, unemployment, the federal debt, and so on. Can those of us who have sat in the locker rooms as our media pundits have declared each victory a fluke, now simply sit in the corner of the stadium hoping that when the team starts losing—one day in a future that never seems to arrive—it will again appreciate our defensive strategies? Or might the team be more appreciative if *we get in the game* today and keep the winning streak going by helping with the problem before it does become a crisis? I believe the last is what the *Economist* and others expect of us. And I know it is what God expects. But that option never *once* entered the mind-set of the special.

Larry Burkett was clear that the Y2K problem is solvable with enough money, people, and time. But he said we aren't making the investment of those resources to solve the problem. Yet conservative American churches are filled with tens of millions of people who have tens of billions of dollars—and enough time in recent years to devote millions of man-hours to political mischief. If we truly believe the Y2K problem is solvable but as potentially serious as the show implied, why haven't we mobilized those resources to keep the problem from becoming a crisis?

In other words, wouldn't it be better to accept the cross, rather than sterno or guns, as the symbol of Christianity, and sacrifice some money, time, and talent for the well-being of our world?

What kind of world would it be if every American responded to every problem of life in the same mind-set, time, and fashion as do some of us in the church? Does our crisis mentality encourage us to *hope* for a disaster, as it will make our job of accomplishing the Great Commission easier? Did Christ refuse to feed the five thousand so they'd get good and hungry and therefore become more receptive to his message? What would Jesus do?

Children sitting beside a peaceful lake will always grow bored and toss a rock just to hear it splash and to watch the waves spread. But as we adults listen to and watch our media personalities who would help us answer—or ignore—life's terribly important questions, we might ponder these recent words from *Christianity Today*:

> Wisdom demands that we become suspicious of celebrities. A big, red "Be Skeptical" sign should flash in our minds whenever we see Christian personalities plastered on our book and magazine covers or hear their smooth voices sweetening our TV's and radios. . . . We need to recognize the painful truth that the pervasiveness of worldly entertainment values within the evangelical subculture has a tendency to minimize the gospel content. . . . Stories continue of egotistical celebrity authors who abuse ghostwriters and publicists, and politics is, well, still politics. Particularly in religious broadcasting and political activism, power and money are often treated as zero-sum games. These "industries" need to pray much about the calling of the Christian in the spotlight.[10]

Even better, we might ask ourselves these questions from God, as God might ask them on Judgement Day:

Is anyone more blind than my servant, more deaf than the messenger I send? Israel, you have seen so much, but what has it meant to you? You have ears to hear with, but what have you really heard?

ISAIAH 42:19–20 GNB

Notes

Introduction

1. *The Forbes Scrapbook of Thoughts on the Business of Life* (Triumph, 1992), 81.

Chapter One

1. Promotional brochure from CBN entitled "Money Management Conference" for October 30–November 2, 1997.

Chapter Two

1. *Economist*, 41.
2. C. S. Lewis, *Mere Christianity,* 81–82.
3. Thomas Merton, *New Seeds of Contemplation* (New Directions, 1961), 48.
4. François Fénelon, *The Royal Way of the Cross* (Paraclete, 1982), 63.
5. Mother Teresa, *Religion and Liberty.*
6. Thomas Merton, *New Seeds,* 47.
7. "The New Outcasts," *Forbes* (August 25, 1997), 52.
8. "The Sorry State of Saving," *Economist* (August 30, 1997), 15.
9. George Bernard Shaw, preface to *Androcles and the Lion.*
10. Aleksandr Solzhenitsyn, *The Gulag Archipelago,* quoted in *One Word of Truth* (Waco, Tex.: Word, 1998).
11. Earl C. Gottschalk Jr., "'Christian' Planners Appear Worldly to Secular Rivals," *Wall Street Journal.*
12. Anita Sharpe, "More Spiritual Leaders Preach Virtue of Wealth," *Wall Street Journal* (April 5, 1996).
13. Michael Novak, *Business As a Calling: Work and the Examined Life* (Free Press, 1997).
14. "The Drama of Willow Creek," *Chicago Daily Herald* (May 19, 1988).
15. *Congregation* (July-August 1996), 4.

16. "In Pursuit of Wealth, Christians Have Forgotten Biblical Teachings," *Philadelphia Inquirer* (January 15, 1997).

Chapter Three

1. "Tobacco Accord Worries Some, but Not Funds," *Wall Street Journal* (June 23, 1997), C1.
2. "Seeing Things As They Really Are," *Forbes* (March 10, 1997), 134, emphasis mine.
3. *Morningstar* report (April 25, 1997), 360.
4. "We're All Bulls Here: Strong Market Makes Everybody an Expert," *Wall Street Journal* (September 12, 1997), A1.
5. "Portfolio 101," *Wall Street Journal* (September 12, 1997), A1.
6. *Outstanding Investor Digest* (August 8, 1997), 12–13.
7. "Tobacco Accord Worries Some, but Not Funds," *Wall Street Journal* (June 23, 1997), C1. Note: Some of the Franklin funds have not followed the same policy as the Templeton funds.
8. "A Real Boycott Takes Sacrifice," *Los Angeles Times* (June 28, 1997), B9.
9. *U.S. News & World Report* (September 15, 1997), 14.
10. *Sarasota Herald Tribune* (September 7, 1997), 1.

Chapter Four

1. Dean Merrill, "How a Lieutenant in the Moral Majority Rediscovered the Power of the Local Church," *Christianity Today* (August 11, 1997), 26.
2. *The Crash: The Coming Financial Collapse of America* (Jeremiah Films), videocassette.
3. Ed Dobson, *The End* (Grand Rapids: Zondervan, 1997), 178.
4. *Christianity Today* (September 1, 1997), 25, emphasis mine.
5. "Pentecostals Redefine Religion in Latin America," *Wall Street Journal* (August 29, 1997), A11.
6. Dobson, *The End* (Grand Rapids: Zondervan, 1997), 180.
7. *Stewardship Matters,* 4, emphasis mine.
8. Bill Bright, "A Serious Countdown," *Campus Crusade* (May-June 1997), 5.
9. *Didache: The Doctrine of the Twelve Apostles,* quoted in *The Treasury of Religious and Spiritual Quotations* (Readers Digest, 1994), 436.

Chapter Five

1. "Pat Robertson, Novelist," *Christianity Today* (September 1, 1997), 25.

2. Ibid.

3. "An American Economy for Americans," *Wall Street Journal* (September 5, 1995), editorial page.

Chapter Six

1. Philip Yancey, *The Jesus I Never Knew* (Grand Rapids: Zondervan, 1995), 72–73.

2. Henri Nouwen.

3. *Religion and Liberty* (November-December 1994), 2–3.

4. *Religion and Liberty* (March-April 1991), 5.

5. *Religion and Liberty* (September-October 1992), 2.

6. Jane Austen, *Pride and Prejudice*.

7. "In Greed We Trust," *Economist* (November 1, 1997), 27.

8. Peter Drucker, *Post-Capitalist Society* (HarperBusiness, 1993), 14.

Chapter Seven

1. Michael E. Porter and Mark Blaxill, *Wall Street Journal* (November 24, 1997), editorial page.

2. *Morningstar* report (August 15, 1997), 147.

3. Ibid., 174.

4. *Morningstar* report (November 7, 1997), 1161.

5. *Morningstar* report (November 21, 1997), 1356.

Chapter Eight

1. "When It's All in the Mind," *U.S. News & World Report* (December 8, 1997), 86.

2. Ibid.

3. "Enough Already," *Forbes* (August 28, 1995), 172.

4. "New Levels in the Stock Market" (August 1929).

5. *Morningstar* summary (February 21, 1998), S32.

6. Ibid., S25.

7. Ibid., S13.

8. Ibid., S24.

9. *Morningstar* report (November 30, 1997).

10. *Morningstar* summary (February 21, 1998), S23.

11. Ibid., S24.

12. *Economist* (October 18, 1997), 79–80.

13. "Asia Shudders at Normal Growth," *Wall Street Journal* (December 5, 1997), international page.

14. "All Fall Down," *Economist* (November 8, 1997), 84.

15. *Morningstar* summary (February 21, 1998), S29.

16. Ibid.

17. *Mutual Funds* (November 1997), 98.

18. *Morningstar* summary (February 21, 1998), S36.

19. "Emerging Triumphant in Foreign Markets," *Smart Money* (November 1997), 35–38.

20. Ibid.

Appendix: Y2K

1. "A Survey of the Millennium Bug," Economist (September 19, 1998), emphasis mine.

2. Ibid., emphasis mine.

3. Paul Kedrosky, "To Figure Out Y2K Hype, Follow the Money," Wall Street Journal (July 20, 1998), editorial page.

4. Donaldson, Lufxii & Jenrethe report (August 7, 1998).

5. "The Y2K Solution: Run for Your Life!" Wired (August 1998), 122.

6. Ibid.

7. Ibid.

8. Ibid.

9. Ibid., emphasis mine.

10. *Christianity Today*

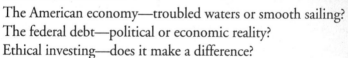

We want to hear from you. Please send your comments about this book
to us in care of the address below. Thank you.

ZondervanPublishingHouse
Grand Rapids, Michigan 49530
http://www.zondervan.com